Spiritual Warfare in the Kingdom of Skullbonia

Spiritual Warfare in the Kingdom of Skullbonia

A Devotional of Short Messages Focused on Spiritual Warfare

Wendell Jellison

Greenfield, Tennessee, USA

Spiritual Warfare in the Kingdom of Skullbonia

Wendell Jellison

Copyright © 2017

Unless otherwise noted, all Scripture references are from the KJV of the Bible.

The cover features the iconic sign at the crossroads in the village of Skullbone, Tennessee.

Graphics by Jeremy Hart for Hart Creative + Design. www.hartcd.com

ISBN: 978-0-9979146-3-4

Printed in USA

About the Author

Wendell Jellison is a native of Portland, Indiana and was ordained by the United Pentecostal Church, Int'l. into the ministry in September 1976.

The Jellison family traveled for twenty-one years as evangelist and gospel singers, and he has been the pastor of three churches in over 20 years of pastoral ministry.

Wendell Jellison is founder and pastor of the First United Pentecostal Church of Greenfield, Tennessee. He is the father to three wonderful daughters and their families that include six beautiful grandchildren.

Contact Information

Wendell Jellison
PO Box 273
Greenfield, TN 38230
731.235.3040

wendelljellison@aol.com

A Note from the Author

These messages are the cumulative result of a lifetime of Bible study and interaction with many people who have impacted my life and ministry. From men who have spoken words into my life of experience and wisdom to authors of books that have influenced my journey, I give thanks to God for the knowledge of Bible salvation, and specifically, enlightenment on spiritual warfare.

Therefore I lay no claim to originality as my life has been influenced by, and now this book reflects, the input of truth from many sources. Phrases or unique thoughts that have become as my own, surely were birthed from hearing a sermon or reading a book at some time in my past. My thanks to all that have shared their passion for truth with this preacher.

Special thanks are due to the late Missionary/Bishop Richard Steve Willoughby of Finley, Tennessee. I approached him some 10 years ago as to his experience with spiritual warfare. He took time to share with me some dynamic thoughts on the subject that started my journey into a deeper understanding of the battle that we faced in the "land between the rivers" in Northwest Tennessee. I am ever so grateful for his guidance on this subject.

Wendell Jellison

Preface

"If my people, which are called by my name, shall humble them-selves, and pray, and seek my face, and turn from their wicked ways; then will I hear from heaven, and will forgive their sin, and will heal their land" (II Chronicles 7:14).

Land has need of healing when there has been no rain. Without the life giving "dew of heaven" the ground becomes dry, hardened and unproductive. There can be no harvest from the seeds that have been planted.

Spiritually, this lack of rain can be attributed to brass ceilings as de-scribed in Deuteronomy 28:15, *"But it shall come to pass, if thou wilt not hearken unto the voice of the LORD thy God, to observe to do all his commandments and his statutes which I command thee this day; that all these curses shall come upon thee, and overtake thee:"* and verse 23, *"And thy heaven that is over thy head shall be brass, and the earth that is under thee shall be iron."*

I believe that Northwest Tennessee, otherwise known as the King-dom of Skullbonia, and many other spiritual territories across our land has experienced a brass ceiling resulting in a spiritual fam-ine such as is noted in the above Scripture. **The land needs to be healed!** Healing will come from an outpouring of spiritual rain that will be manifest in a mighty Holy Ghost revival in this time of the end. For that healing to come, there must be humility, prayer, seek-ing the face of God and the actual turning away from sin. Then God will hear the prayers of desperate people! He will forgive their sin and He will heal their land! **When the land is healed, the precious seeds of the gospel message that have been sowed with tears over many years will suddenly break through the soil and the Church will gather many souls into the Kingdom of God.**

That is what this book is all about.

Here is a collection of messages that I have preached on the radio in this battle for spiritual victory in Northwest Tennessee. I have cho-sen sermons of faith, prayer, sound doctrine, spiritual intercession, sins of the land, generational curses and others that are vital to the spiritual warfare that we are fighting.

Most Christian churches operate in the spiritual atmosphere of New Testament Nazareth: because of unbelief Jesus could do no mighty work there *"...save that he laid his hands upon a few sick folk, and healed them"* (Mark 6:5). Some churches have success in getting a few sick folk healed, but few see the mighty works that are promised in the Word of God.

Again, that's what this book is all about.

There is healing for the land and with that healing will come a great harvest of souls!

Wendell Jellison

Introduction

"For we wrestle not against flesh and blood, but against principalities, against powers, against the rulers of the darkness of this world, against spiritual wickedness in high places" (Ephesians 6:12).

On December 27, 1952, Tennessee Governor Gordon Browning made a proclamation that the land between the Tennessee and Mississippi rivers in Northwest Tennessee would be known as the Kingdom of Skullbonia in reference to the colorful history of the area. One historian wrote that the Wild West was tame compared to Skullbonia. The area was widely known for vices such as bare-knuckle boxing (to the skull only), gang warfare, prostitution, the KKK, illegal gambling, etc. Greenfield is located near the center of the Kingdom of Skullbonia, actually 7 miles northwest of the village of Skullbone, from which the name originates.

So, I surmise the name of our regional adversary who serves under Satan in evil strongholds throughout our area might be the "Prince of the Kingdom of Skullbonia." (In Daniel chapter 10 we read of the prince of Persia and the prince of Grecia). Regardless, there is great spiritual warfare taking place for the souls of men and women. There is a famine of spiritual hunger all around us. It's necessary to pray that God will remove spiritual blindness from people so that they can be saved! People believe in God, but few want to serve him, except upon their own terms. And, that's not going to work on Judgment Day! Jesus said in John 14:15, *"If ye love me, keep my commandments."*

Now, notice this with me. God not only deals with individuals, but throughout the Bible, God dealt with cities, regions and nations. Notice the reference to cities such as Nineveh, Sodom and Gomorrah, Jerusalem, and many, many others. **Every community or region has its own spiritual identity.** And, many communities today are known by their prominent sin. Some cities have been known as murder capitals. Las Vegas carries the dubious title of sin city. San Francisco is the gay capital of America. New Orleans has always been noted for its Mardi Gras celebrations and as a gathering place for witchcraft and the occult while touting Bourbon Street for its perversions. And, locally, communities are often known for gangs, drugs or wild night life. **Prominent sins of a community or a particular region can bind spiritual victory until spiritual warfare breaks through the barriers that such sin, abominations, idolatry, or whatever, has built.**

Until passionate, concerned Christians wage spiritual warfare against the powers of the air that control certain areas, revival will never be widespread, and spiritual renewals will be short lived. Even before I fully understood this truth, I experienced it as an evangelist just by crossing state lines or going into different areas. Although demographics were much the same and the people were of the same culture, just crossing a state line could make all the difference in the world in how a revival would turn out. I could preach a message in one state and have wonderful results. Then I could travel a few miles away and preach the same message in a different church in a different state, and get few results; a tougher time, a difficult anointing. Why? Spiritual warfare had not broken through those barriers in the second state or region.

In the mid 1980's a great Pentecostal revival swept through our eastern states, right up the coast into the Northeast. Prior to that time, that area was a difficult place to preach in, and evangelists in the 1970's often had few results. Crowds were small, churches were struggling but, something happened and, to this day, there is a breakthrough and there are great revival churches throughout the east all because someone, somewhere, broke through the barriers with much prayer, fasting, passion, and a genuine desperation for a Holy Ghost revival. I've preached in several of those cities over the years and pastors well remember the years of struggle, and then the years of revival, not only in their particular assembly, but throughout their region.

I believe that God has a mighty Holy Ghost outpouring planned for the region of Northwest Tennessee in **the Kingdom of Skullbonia.**

As you go through these messages you will read about a prayer walk. This is in reference to our ongoing daily prayer walk through the downtown area of our community that members of our church have been doing since June 16, 2005. We pray for our city and are active in binding and loosing (see Matthew 18:18) as we pray for a mighty outpouring of the Holy Ghost in our town and throughout Northwest Tennessee.

This collection of messages has been broadcast by Thunderbolt Broadcasting WCDZ FM95.1 in Martin, Tennessee during our 7:30 a.m. CDT Sunday morning program which was started on January 1, 2005, and continues to this day. Live streaming of the broadcast is available at www.thunderboltbroadcasting.com and on mobile devices through the Thunderbolt Broadcasting app. The messages have been edited for publication.

Chapter Titles

Dedication

This book is dedicated to the inmates that I have had the privilege of praying with and baptizing in the name of our Lord Jesus Christ in Northwest Tennessee jails through the ministries of Veneda Ing and Betty Hodge. The inmates' struggles with broken lives, drug and alcohol addiction, shattered self-esteem, abuse of all kinds and their innate desire to find God has driven and inspired me to persevere in spiritual battles in the "land between the rivers." I want to encourage and strengthen those who have been trapped in cultures of perversion, immorality, or godless influence. Jesus thought they deserved better. I do too.

Thanks

My sincere thanks to Llynn Enmen, Amy Davidson and Darla Andrews for their expertise in proofreading and editing. Their advice and hours of labor have made this work possible.

Be Thou Made Whole

When one of the ten lepers returned to give Jesus thanks for healing him of his leprosy, Jesus said this to him. *"Arise, go thy way; thy faith hath made thee whole"* (Luke 17:19).

Commentators agree that the nine lepers were cleansed of their leprosy; but this man, who came back to give God thanks, was not only cleansed of his leprosy but was made whole. His body, soul and spirit were made whole. He was a changed man. Not just healed physically, but made whole.

If you are a believer, have you been made whole? If you are a born again Christian can you also say that you have been made whole? Has God really touched you physically, spiritually and emotionally? Are you made whole?

I have seen many people who have professed to be born again, Spirit-filled believers, yet have obviously not been made whole. Is it all right if I just be honest and open with you? It's a problem that many are facing. Saved? Yes. Born again? Yes. Spirit filled? Yes. But, made whole, maybe not! That ought not to be. My God is able to make us whole, That is God's plan through His atoning work at Calvary.

There are nine references in the New Testament to where Jesus caused people to be made whole! A person is made up of a spirit, soul and body. In I Thessalonians 5:23 we read, *"And the very God of peace sanctify you wholly; and I pray God your whole spirit and soul and body be preserved blameless unto the coming of our Lord Jesus Christ."*

He will do what? *Yes,* **He will preserve your spirit, soul and body!**

Jesus not only healed the Canaanite woman's daughter physically, but her daughter was made whole from that very hour.

When the woman with the issue of blood touched the hem of His garment she was made whole.

I like Mark 6:56, *"And whithersoever he entered, into villages, or cities, or country, they laid the sick in the streets, and besought him that they might touch if it were but the border of his garment: and as many as touched him were made whole."*

If you are still struggling with sin, you need to be delivered and made whole.

If you are sick, you need to claim your wholeness.

If you have been born again, but still struggle with depression, you need to stand on the Word and be made whole.

Sad to say, but, just being honest, I've seen people baptized and filled with the Holy Ghost, and still struggle with alcohol, cigarettes, illegal drugs, depression, you name it. Folks, that ought not to be! I am preaching a word of faith to you. By the authority of the name of Jesus Christ, be made whole; body, soul and spirit!

I don't know when the term bi-polar came into use, but it seems to me that people who have been diagnosed with being bi-polar or manic depression, feel that God doesn't heal that kind of thing. I've got good news for you. I have the Word of God that tells me that people that are manic depressive can be made whole! Set free by the miraculous healing power of God! **It is God's will that you be healed!** That your mind be at peace! That wild mood swings become a thing of the past! God is still God! There is healing and wholeness in the name of Jesus. Go ahead, shout it out. "I am made whole!"

Don't be satisfied with less than wholeness in every area of your life.

Before the Still Small Voice

In I Kings chapter 19, we read of an interesting experience that the prophet Elijah had. He had just had his great encounter with King Ahab and the prophets of Baal on Mt. Carmel where God had come through again!

Then, Queen Jezebel sends him a message that she would have him killed within 24 hours. This previously brave man of God runs scared and hides in a cave trying to save his life. Elijah was depressed; having a bad day. He was running for his life. Ever been there? He needed a word from God! Elijah needed direction. He needed encouragement. And sure enough, God came through; He always does. But, we need to read the rest of the story.

Before the still, small voice came from God there was a great and strong wind that broke the rocks on the mountain. Now that's a powerful storm. We're talking about rocks being split and rock-slides crashing down the side of the mountain. This was surely a terrifying experience. By application we're talking about homes breaking up and marriages splitting. Children being tossed about. Perhaps even experiences like abuse and perversion. Things that destroy homes and security. That's not exactly what Elijah was praying for! Likewise, **while you are waiting on a word from the Lord, it sometimes seems that all you can see is destruction taking place.**

But that wasn't the worst. When the wind died down and the rocks finally settled, then an earthquake struck! An earthquake shakes your foundation. An earthquake makes you unstable, maybe even a feeling of dizziness! Ever experienced an earthquake in your life? I'm not talking about a natural one; I'm talking about one in your life. Sure you have. All the while, you feel just like Elijah. God, I need a word. I need encouragement; not an earthquake!

If that wasn't enough, then there was a fire! An uncontrolled fire destroys things. Maybe you've been there, too: life destroyed; finances destroyed; relationships destroyed. Perhaps today you are actually in the process of picking your way through the ashes to see what's left of your life. Perhaps for the last several days or weeks you've experienced the wind, the earthquake and then the fire in your life.

I have good news for you! After all of the elements had their way, **God showed up!**

Sometimes, and to be honest, many times, God allows the wind, the earthquakes, and the fires to do their thing and then He shows up just to prove that He can put the pieces back together and make something beautiful out of the ashes of our lives.

Often, the wind, the earthquakes and the fire are the results of seeds that we have planted, and we are actually harvesting what we have sown. I have found that a vast majority of the things that I have faced in life have been the result of seeds that I have planted in one way or the other.

Thank God for the rest of the story, *"And, after the fire, a still small voice"* (I Kings 19:12). God began to speak to the discouraged, depressed prophet with hope and a new direction for his life.

I'm just trying to show you that if you are waiting on a word from God, hang tough through the stuff that life brings you—**you WILL hear from God!** He will come to you with encouragement and a new direction. The stress and the struggles that you have been through do not mean that God isn't going to answer. He's coming. Keep your faith. Can you say this prayer with me? "God, I'm waiting on your help. And, with your help, I know I will make it through what I'm going through. And, soon, I expect to hear from You with the answers that I need in my life. Amen."

Understanding God's Will For Your Life

I want to share something with you that has affected my life in a very strong measure. The will of God is absolutely necessary for a person to be effective in living, in marriage, in raising a family, in fulfilling a calling, and having the assurance of spiritual power and authority in our lives. Knowing that you are walking in God's will releases faith in any situation and brings assurance in times of testing.

We know, of course, that **obedience to the law of God is a requirement for us to walk in God's will**. Many Scriptures bear out this truth.

Having said that, we all can go through tough times where we spend time trying to be sure that we are in God's will. We seek God's will because we sometimes feel that this trouble I'm in cannot be God's will; so I must find it somewhere else. Well, first of all, **God's will can put us right in the middle of problems.** God's will can be that we are suffering for Him.

Or, God's will can be that we are reaping what we've sown and God is trying to show us changes that need to be made in our character, in our attitude, in our walk with God, or in our relationship with people.

Sometimes it's a job situation, an income problem, or, a personality conflict on the job. There are many reasons why we may be seeking God's will for our life.

Author Henry Blackaby in his book *Experiencing God* makes this point concerning praying for God's will: "What is God's will for my life? [This question] is not the right question. The right question is, What is God's will?" In other words, we just need God's will for today, not our whole lives. If we know God's will for today, we can adjust our lives according to His will today and His will for our lives will unfold accordingly—one day at a time.

Let me put it this way. If you will seek God's will today, your to-morrows will take care of themselves. We can get so focused on the future that we fail to see how important today is. Too many times we are thinking of doing better when God's will is found. I will pray more then. When things get straightened out in my life, then I will pray, fast and be faithful in my walk with God.

Well, friend, you'll never get your life straightened that way. **Walking in God's will today is the first and most important step of finding God's will tomorrow.**

I've seen men and women who feel they have a God-called ministry; but, they can't use their gifts where they're at. They feel they need to move away; go somewhere else, and then they can be effective. It never happens that way. I'm not saying that there aren't certain fields of labor where a ministry might flourish better than others, but to do nothing today, waiting on tomorrow, is not God's will. He expects us to use the gifts and talents we have today and He will take care of tomorrow.

I can't emphasize too much what I feel about this message. Our focus needs to be on God, not on our life. Don't take that to mean that you shouldn't be diligent about living. You must be. But, if you are stalemated, stuck, not going anywhere, can't get certain prayers answered, could it not be that you are focused on God's will for your life, when you just need to find God's will for today?!

When God told Noah to build an ark, Noah didn't have all the details about what was getting ready to take place. God saw the big picture.

Judgment was coming to the world, and God was ready to destroy the human race when Noah found grace in the eyes of the Lord. So God had to find a way to save Noah and his family. Noah couldn't see the whole picture. He could not have realized all that God was doing and how he was going to be used to save the human race from extinction. All he knew was that he needed to build an ark to be in God's will today.

Abraham couldn't see all of God's will for his life. All he could see was that God had told him to leave his family and go to a land that God would show him. God gave him promises but no details. Abraham was counted righteous because of his obedience to the Word of God.

It doesn't matter to me what the future holds. As long as I am in the will of God today, God will take care of my tomorrows.

Worry, depression, and many emotional problems are often the result of trying to live out the future when we need to live out the day.

If you want God's blessings; if you want peace of mind; if you want spiritual power; this lesson must be learned. Problems can overwhelm us. Difficulties can almost swallow us. Friends can forsake us. Grief can be overbearing. Depression can be mind-numbing. Sickness can be devastating. Loneliness can be painful. The answer is to put your future in the hands of God and live for Him today.

From Bethany to Jerusalem

I witnessed to a woman once that felt that because she had received a miraculous healing she was saved. She didn't need any more of God in her life. She had received a miracle so that was enough. She did not go to church. She felt secure that God's grace was applied to her life and she was safe from hell because of the time when she had received a miracle of healing.

Let me remind you of Christ's ascension at Bethany. Forty days after His resurrection some 500 people stood on the side of the Mt. of Olives at Bethany and received a blessing from the Lord. He then ascended into the heavens. While the people stood, looking up into the heavens two angels appeared with this message, "... *why stand ye gazing up into heaven? this same Jesus, which is taken up from you into heaven, shall so come in like manner as ye have seen him go into heaven*" (Acts 1:11).

So, Christ's second coming was again confirmed, and we wait, expectantly, for that to happen in our lifetime.

But there was more. **That group of 500 people were told to go into Jerusalem and wait for the promise of the Father, the infilling of the Holy Ghost**. We know that with that experience came the sermon from Peter that confirmed the fulfillment of Christ's command to Nicodemus in John chapter 3:3, "*Ye must be born again.*"

Peter preached to the crowd at Pentecost in Acts 2:38, "...*repent, and be baptized every one of you in the name of Jesus Christ for the remission of sins, and ye shall receive the gift of the Holy Ghost."* This became the normal experience for converts in the early church.

What happened to the 380 that didn't go on to the upper room? What happened to the 380 that didn't see the importance of continuing on to obey the command of the Lord? I fear lest the same thing that happened to them has happened to a host of professing Christians today.

The 500 became believers at Bethany but only 120 were filled with the Spirit. I'm sure that everyone one of them believed on the Lord Jesus Christ. He was real. He resurrected from the dead. He was alive. They believed in the death, the burial, and resurrection of the Lord. They had been blessed, the Scripture said, by the Lord, but, they weren't saved. The Holy Ghost had not yet been given. They had been instructed in Luke 24:49 to "*tarry ye in the city of Jerusalem until you be endued with power from on high."* Which was the promise of the Father: God in us.

They had been beneficiaries of grace, God's unmerited favor. **But folks, don't make the mistake that grace is salvation. No, grace is the vehicle that brings you to salvation.** It is the path that takes you to salvation, but grace is not salvation.

Notice Titus 2:11, "*For the grace of God that **bringeth** salvation hath appeared to all men, 12 **Teaching** us that, denying ungodliness and worldly lusts, we should live soberly, righteously, and godly, in this present world;"*

The grace of God brings salvation by teaching us how to live for God. Some confuse the works of the law with the works of righteousness. Works of the law can't save you. But, when you come to salvation, there will be works of righteousness that allow God's grace to bring salvation to you such as: repentance, perhaps even restitution, your water baptism and your new life of personal holiness, with its do's and don'ts. Those are works of righteousness, not works of law.

There are many who literally worship grace. These are the people who are dependent upon grace to save them because they recognize that they don't live their life for God. They're just hoping the Lord's grace will take them to heaven when they die. I'm afraid, by the Scriptures, that they have a sad day coming. The grace of God brings a person to salvation but is not salvation in itself.

If you want to be saved you will follow the plan of salvation and go on from Bethany to Jerusalem, from believing to being born again. From believing to being filled with the Spirit! What a difference!

Belief

A young woman walked into the Clothing Exchange, our unofficial church outreach center that is camouflaged as my daughter Lana's consignment shop. The woman told my daughter that she was to have surgery to remove a brain tumor in a few days. Another lady from our church walked in and at that moment there were no other customers in the store. So, Lana, myself and our church member— all three Spirit-filled believers—prayed for her healing.

The next day, when this woman with the brain tumor went to the doctor for preparation for her surgery, there was no brain tumor! Gone! Now, some four months later that tumor is still gone. Doctors can't explain such a thing; but we can. In obedience to the Word of God, and through the prayer of faith, God healed that brain tumor.

Upon sharing the account of this miracle with a young man, he asked me this question. **"Do you really believe that you had influence on that tumor disappearing?"** I answered, "Absolutely!" He asked if it couldn't have been just a coincidence, to which I replied, "No, it was obviously in answer to prayer!" I even stated it this way. **"I don't believe that that woman would've been healed if we hadn't prayed**." She would've had brain surgery."

A Bible-believing child of God has both authority and power with God.

I give God all of the honor and all of the glory. Yes, it is in response to the faith and obedience of the person praying, but no human being can heal anyone. I can't heal anyone, but I can pray and in obedience to the Word of God, I can see God respond to my prayers! When God uses a person to affect a miracle of any kind, it's a very humbling experience causing a realization of how mighty God is!

Let me give you another example. A few years ago I was driving into Jackson, TN, from Tupelo, MS, when I received a phone call that a 13 year old girl was at the point of death in the Jackson hospital. I didn't know the young girl or her family, but someone from our church knew of the situation and placed the call to me. I felt the witness of the Holy Spirit that I should go and pray, so I went to the hospital late in the evening, met the family, and we prayed together. The girl had been comatose for several hours. As soon as we prayed, she awakened, opened her eyes, looked around, and started talking to her mother and father. She went home the next day, healed by the power of God through the prayers of someone who dared to believe that God would answer prayer! A few days later I met the young lady at our church-owned retail shop. A divine miracle! Would that have happened if someone hadn't prayed? No. **Believers are the voice, the hands, the feet, and the love of God to this hurting world.**

I am challenging someone to dare to believe God! Jesus told the father with the lunatic son, in Mark 9:23, *"If thou canst believe, all things are possible to him that believeth."*

To the centurion who had a servant sick of the palsy, Jesus said in Matthew 8:13, *"And Jesus said unto the centurion, Go thy way; and as thou hast believed, so be it done unto thee. And his servant was healed in the selfsame hour."*

In Matthew 9, Jesus touched the eyes of two blind men, but notice what He said, AFTER he touched them, (verse 29) *"According to your faith be it unto you. And their eyes were opened!"* Notice again, He touched them, but it was according to their faith!

The power of UNBELIEF is clearly seen when Jesus visited His own hometown of Nazareth. **He couldn't do any mighty works**

there because of unbelief. The Word says in Mark 6:5, *"And he could there do no mighty work, save that he laid his hands upon a few sick folk, and healed them."*

I am speaking to some today who are so filled with unbelief that God can do no mighty work in your life. Unbelief kills the operation of faith. Unbelief ties the hand of God. Unbelief hinders the will of God from being done. Unbelief allows the works of darkness to bring sickness, fear, worry, depression, division, and even death into people's lives. **"God, grant us a revival of faith and fresh belief in the power of God to do what Your Word says You will do."**

If Thou Canst Believe

Faith is not generally the problem with people getting their prayers answered. Faith gets you praying. Faith brings hope for healing and deliverance. *"Now faith is the substance of things hoped for, the evidence of things not seen"* (Hebrews 11:1). Many people here in the Bible belt have faith. Even a little bit is enough to please God, for He said in Matthew 17:20, *"If ye have faith as a grain of mustard seed, ye shall say unto this mountain, Remove hence to yonder place; and it shall remove; and nothing shall be impossible unto you."* So, a little bit of faith that God will answer your prayers is enough to move a problem that appears like a mountain to you!

So, why don't we get more prayers answered? The real culprit is doubt.

After Jesus rescued Peter from drowning, after having walked on the water, notice what happens. *"And immediately Jesus stretched forth his hand, and caught him, and said unto him, O thou of little faith, wherefore didst thou doubt?"* (Matthew 14:31). Peter's little faith allowed him to walk on the water! But Peter looked at the situation and began to doubt! *"But when he saw the wind boisterous, he was afraid; and beginning to sink, he cried, saying, Lord, save me"* (Matthew 14:30). He was already getting his miracle, when he began to doubt. He started to notice the strong wind; the high waves. He took his eyes off of the Lord. And, when he did, doubt settled in and he must've begun to think, "I can't do this! This is

25

impossible!" I don't really know what he was thinking, but the Lord had to rescue him, and asked him, *"…wherefore didst thou doubt?"* (Matthew 14:31).

Doubt is the problem that many people have. For many people, faith is not the issue. Doubt is. Can you have both? Of course, look what the father in Mark 9:24 said, *"I believe. Help thou mine unbelief!"* I believe, but I don't believe! I believe in God, but I don't believe He can do this for me! Or, perhaps, I believe that God can do this, but surely not for me! I'm not worthy. I'm not ready. I'm not perfect. I'm not good enough. So, yes, part of me believes. But another part throws in doubt and fear. When that happens, I tie the hand of God and I don't get my miracle, or, I get a partial miracle, or, the miracle isn't permanent.

To doubt is to judge. **To have doubt about your faith is to judge yourself outside of the grace of God.**

Have you ever said, "God will heal me when He gets ready?" You are really saying that you don't believe in the power of prayer, in the power of binding and loosing, or in the Word of God that says, *"By His stripes we are healed"* (Isa. 53:5). Instead, you are saying, "I believe God CAN heal, but I don't expect it now." So, you judge yourself as ineligible at this time. Or, you say, "Well, I know God CAN, but I'm not worthy," thereby, judging yourself again, ineligible, and again tying the hand of God.

When crowds came to Jesus, He didn't divide them into groups and decide which ones were ready now, those who were worthy now, or those who had suffered enough. No, He just healed them all! Right then! All of them!

God, forgive us for our unbelief!

Spiritual Breakthrough

We need spiritual breakthrough when we face battles that we cannot overcome like fear that won't go away or a past that we can't get over. We need spiritual breakthrough when we can't feel victory, peace, joy, contentment, or love. We need a spiritual breakthrough when we aren't free to worship. When we just can't pray like we know we should, we need spiritual breakthrough. When we're not free to love, or to give ourselves and our possessions to the work of God, we need spiritual breakthrough. If we are in bondage to fear, anger, depression, sinful behavior, or sinful thoughts, we need spiritual breakthrough. We need spiritual breakthrough when we are bound, walled in, shut out, or when we don't enjoy the presence of God like we sing or preach about. When we can't find God or when our testimony has grown cold and ineffective, we need spiritual breakthrough. When church attendance becomes a thing that we can live with or without, we need spiritual breakthrough. When fellowship with God's people is no longer important to us, we need spiritual breakthrough. When we do things that we know we shouldn't be doing, but seemingly have no power to change or overcome habitual sin, we need spiritual breakthrough.

We need spiritual breakthrough when we live in condemnation of our lifestyle, but don't have the will power to change and do the right thing. When we watch bad TV programs, videos, and Internet and don't have the will power to turn it off, and we don't even feel too guilty, we need spiritual breakthrough. When we excuse our sin with, "It didn't hurt anything," we need spiritual breakthrough. When ungodly music and entertainment brings no conviction of wrongdoing, we need spiritual breakthrough.

Are you in bondage? Are you in need of a spiritual breakthrough? Do any of the things I've just listed fit you and your situation?

A spiritual breakthrough will come only through a spiritual battle. You're going to have to engage the enemy in spiritual warfare. You're going to have to do something about your situation. You can sit there until you literally die, and be bound with the same problems, same hang-ups, same sins, same problems, same guilt and never find deliverance if you don't do something about it!

The Prophets Jeremiah and Hosea both cried out *"break up your fallow ground."* Get back on your prayer bones! Humble yourself under the mighty hand of God. **Seek God. You will find Him. That's a promise!**

Breakthroughs into greater faith and a deeper walk with God don't just happen! You must seek them. God wants you to have peace of mind. He wants you to be free to seek Him. He wants you to be free to worship Him. He wants you to be strong spiritually, physically and emotionally.

You've been stuck behind your wall of sin, guilt, failure, fears, and hurt far too long. It's time for a breakthrough. Victory is on the other side of that wall in your life.

That promised breakthrough comes through a touch from God Almighty as you make up your mind to obey His Word! That promised breakthrough comes as the result of sincere repentance for failing God while in your bondage.

Let me pray for you right now. "God, You see every one that You are dealing with, and particularly the one who has been offended. The offense is still fresh and it hurts to think about it. This person has been bound by this offense far too long. Be free! Through the mighty name of Jesus Christ, be free from this bondage. I release a spiritual breakthrough In Jesus' name!" Thank God for the victory!

Between a Rock and a Hard Place

In I Samuel 11, the men of Jabesh were given an ultimatum. They could either surrender and have their right eyes thrust out or die. In other words they could live only under the condition that they would live as a reproach upon their nation, and thereby upon their God. Remember, that all nations had their own gods that they worshiped, but Israel served the only true and living God. Their enemies wanted to bring a reproach upon Israel's God.

The church's enemy loves to use anything he can to bring a reproach upon the children of God. The men of Jabesh were between a rock and a hard place. They had only two very unpleasant choices. Either choice they made was not going to end up in a good way. Perhaps you have been there. Perhaps you're there today. You are between a rock and a hard place.

Maybe the job that you have doesn't pay enough to meet the bills; but you don't have a better job to go to, and can't get off work to go find one. You're between a rock and a hard place; can't afford the medicine and can't live without it. Don't have enough money to fix the car and still pay the electric bill this month. But, if you don't fix the car you lose the job. If you don't pay the utility bills your wife and babies won't have any heat, no refrigerator, no gas for the cook stove. What to do? Which way do you turn?

Satan is real good at getting us caught between a rock and a hard place and wearing out our minds, messing up our thoughts and making us miserable.

The Ammonites had come against Jabesh and they didn't have a chance. They begged for mercy and said "We will serve you just let us make a covenant together." But, the covenant was to have their right eyes put out! So, the men of Jabesh asked for seven days to see if they could find help and they sent messengers to King Saul and asked if there was any one to help.

Notice this. Their enemy allowed them to send for help. It seems to me that Satan just wasn't smart here. Why would he allow them to go get help? When you get caught between a rock and a hard place, go for help! Look to the Lord! The devil can't keep your prayers from getting through. **The angels of the Lord are mighty messengers and if you're in a tight spot today, just let the devil know that all you need is a little more time,** and help will be on the way!

Let me encourage someone today! You may seem stuck between decisions with no good answer available. Any way you turn you're going to fail. Do what the men of Jabesh did. Send for help!

How do you do that? First of all, pray and ask God for mercy. His mercies are fresh every morning! You can start over today! You may not see any way out, but He sees a lot more than you do, and many times in my life God has turned an impossible situation into a completely different situation than what I had imagined.

A person that's between a rock and a hard place also needs a person of faith to minister to him or her. A man or woman of God can impart a word of confidence and surety into a situation and that kind of faith can change the future of anyone.

When you call for help, guess what happens? Look what happened in this Bible story. King Saul sent messengers with the good news that 330,000 men were on their way! Notice again, the enemy couldn't stop the messengers from getting through the enemy lines.

It is my goal to help you today. I am a messenger sent to you, and though Satan doesn't want you to hear this message, he can't stop you from hearing it. Stop what you are doing and lift up your hands and voice to the Lord and begin to praise Him that the message of hope got through to you. I know you don't see the answer yet, but the answer is on the way! **When you don't know which way to turn, just turn to God.**

Repentance may be required on your behalf. I don't know how you've been living. If you haven't been faithful to God, you will need to put forth an effort to show that you're willing to change. If you have never been born again, you need to get some things right between you and your God. But, friend, God loves you and He is willing to send in reinforcements.

Chaos Brings Order—Part 1

In Philippians 4:19 we read, *"But my God shall supply all your need according to his riches in glory by Christ Jesus."* The Word of God is true. Since God said that He would supply my needs, then I believe He will. However, I have also lived long enough and experienced enough to know that there have been times when it didn't seem like God was fulfilling His Word in my life. There have been times when it was obvious that I had needs that were not being met. Financially, emotionally...whatever. Perhaps you have faced that same dilemma. You have faced impossible situations and God just wasn't showing up with an answer.

While I've experienced some of these tough times, I can likewise speak with authority to tell you that God's Word is true. Our way of thinking and God's way of thinking are different. Isaiah 55:8, *"For my thoughts are not your thoughts, neither are your ways my ways, saith the LORD."*

Chaos can bring a new order to your life if you will keep your faith in God

When confusion, despair, and unpredictable events come into your life, it's time to seek God; not run from Him. God is not trying to destroy you; He's trying to make you into His likeness. My thought comes from author Chuck Pierce in his book *Interpreting the Times,* where he states that "All organisms of life live in perfect balance

33

and harmony. Our wilderness experiences produce new order in our lives".

He further states, "The Israelites' forty years of wilderness wanderings reordered a people so that the generation of unbelief was removed. Do not fear your wilderness; let the Lord reorder your life and remove everything that will hinder your future."

Our tendency for foolishness is strongest when we are afraid or insecure. Someone once said that faith is neither proven nor real until it is tested, and one cannot give testimony until there is a test. Abraham, the father of the faithful and the friend of God, experienced the testing of God many times in his journey of faith. His faith was tested but he ultimately experienced the fulfillment of the promises of God.

In other words, **God allows chaos to come into our lives to bring new order to us.** We want new order. We need major changes. We want things to be different. But, we naturally resist change. The way that you are headed is the way you are going to go. **So, for things to change, something must change.**

Lifestyle upsets, or chaos, often brings us the changes that we need but were unable to affect by ourselves.

If I asked you what your greatest need is, what would you say: more money, better kids or more loving spouse, or better job? These are legitimate needs, but for an example, often we need to change our spending habits before God will send more money. Also, kids grow up to be the sum and total of what we have put into them in their childhood, so be careful in blaming them for all of their actions. Often, the parents need to change.

Do you desire a more loving spouse? Perhaps the question should be, "Do YOU know how to fulfill the needs of your spouse?" What about a better job? What are your work habits? Do you have the respect of your employer? Or, have you ruined chances for an increase in pay because of rash actions, hot temper, or even drug abuse?

On the other hand the real need we have may be to learn how to love. Maybe unforgiveness is the stumbling block. Do you know the importance of forgiving those who offend you? Have you learned the value of giving? How about the importance of faithfulness?

On the subject of need and God supplying all of your needs, are you listening for God's voice in the midst of your chaos, your wilderness? Is God trying to talk to you? Are you listening? Are you able to hear His voice?

Often, what we think of as our greatest need is not really the need, but just a symptom of our real need. So when chaos comes, and it will to all of us at times in our lives, instead of jumping ship, leaving the family, quitting church, changing jobs irresponsibly, or even blaming God, realize that throughout the Bible God brought new order into people's future through the chaos of the present.

Remember Joseph who was sold into slavery and ended up being the governor of Egypt and saving his family from starvation. Remember Job who kept his faith, declaring *"though he slay me yet will I trust in him"* (Job 13:15) and he ended up twice blessed! The ultimate example; **the chaos of Christ's death brought life for every human being who will believe and obey the gospel of Jesus Christ.**

God's order can come out of Satan's chaos!

Chaos Brings Order—Part 2

Smith Wigglesworth was a preacher who lived during the late 1800's and early 1900's. In the book titled *"Apostle of Faith"* he is quoted as saying, **"I am not moved by what I see or hear; I am moved by what I believe."** That statement is a strong one in that it is a firm commitment to God's Word! This kind of faith is the kind of faith that will move mountains. Faith like that will calm troubled seas. Faith like that will enable God to work through a person to see signs, wonders and miracles by Jesus Christ!

We are too often motivated, impacted, and often depressed by what we see and hear. When in reality, God's Word tells us plainly in Philippians 4:19, *"But my God shall supply all your need according to his riches in glory by Christ Jesus."* If you can believe that verse, you have everything you need today. Period! That settles it! You have the precious Word of God on your side. **If you needed it, you'd have had it. If not, you'll get it when you need it.** Can you believe that?

God's Word says plainly in Romans 8:28, *"And we know that all things work together for good to them that love God, to them who are the called according to his purpose".* **Everything that happens is not good, but God will bring good out of it, if you will believe that all things work together for good.** Can you believe those words?

Can you believe the promises of God when trouble comes into your life? When confusion, despair and unpredictable events come into your life, can you still believe the Word?

Let me help you to understand. God doesn't cause the chaos, but when He allows it to come into our lives, He will bring a new order into our life through the chaos. ALL things work together for good, IF you will keep your integrity and faith in God. **God will bring a new order into your life through the chaos you're going through.**

What am I talking about? Perhaps the death of a loved one, sickness, disease, pain, financial ruin, or loss of a job has brought chaos into your life for a season. We often need new order in our life but are unable or unwilling to implement the change ourselves. We want things to be different. We want things to be better. We may need major changes in our lifestyle, our priorities, our jobs or our faith.

Just look back on your life. You will see where horrible things, chaos, and other lifestyle upsets, often resulted in significant changes in your life that were, actually, in the long run, a better way, a better lifestyle, and even resulted in a better home.

I experienced this kind of new order when I was drafted into the army during the Vietnam War. At that time, it was the worst possible thing that could've happened to me. I was sure it was not God's will that I serve in the army! I prayed and prayed to that end. But Uncle Sam did call. I served my country in Germany and came home two years later a better and more mature man. As I look back on that time, I wouldn't trade that military experience for anything. Out of chaos in my life, God brought a new order into my life. And, actually, it was during that time in Germany that I first walked into a Pentecostal church service. That has changed my life until this very day!

We often don't know what we really need in our life. We pray for a particular need, but in reality we need something else much worse. We think we need more money when we really need better spending and saving habits. We think we need emotional healing when we really need an attitude change. We think we need better friends, when we need to be a better friend to the ones we have.

I've seen people get mad at God because they lost their job when in reality it was their hot temper and disrespect for authority that cost them their job. Don't lose your faith during a chaotic time. You'll come out better in the long run if you'll be like Job and say, *"Though he slay me yet will I trust in Him"* (Job 13:15).

Remember Joseph who was sold into slavery and ended up being the governor of Egypt and saved his family from starvation. Throughout the Bible we see stories of how, through chaos, God brought new order into people's future through the chaos of the present.

What are you going through today?

Let's start by telling God we're sorry for complaining and being impatient. Go ahead. Do it now. "God, I'm sorry for complaining about my problem. I should know better. You're in charge. Please forgive me for my impatience. I repent before you now! God I will trust you to bring needed order into my life. I'm starting a new walk of faith right now. I believe that You, God, will bring new order into my life through this trial that I'm going through. Amen."

Reach out by faith! Let faith minister to you right now. Maybe it's a looming divorce. Maybe it's a doctor's report of sickness or disease that's got you really down. Maybe it's a job situation. Perhaps you can't see a way out. **Put your faith in God. He will bring you through, every time, on time!**

Gideon

God's will—that's a phrase that most of us have used in our conversations. God's will—when we say that, we are inferring that first of all, there is an all-knowing and an all-powerful God that can and does intervene in our human lives. And, if you believe that there is a God, His will becomes important: finding God's will, submitting to God's will, praying for God's will, searching for God's will. I want God's will in my life and I don't want to become guilty of hindering or frustrating God's will in my life by living contrary to His commandments as revealed in the Bible.

But, with all of that said, it seems that life can bring us to places where we feel inadequate, or undersupplied, or robbed of the capability to perform God's will. Maybe through sickness you feel that you can't do what God wants you to do. Or through a broken marriage, you can't fulfill God's will in your life. Or through inadequate finances you are hindered from accomplishing the dreams that you thought God had given you. Maybe a lack of education keeps you from certain levels of leadership. Or a fractured relationship has severed a connection you needed for success. To a called man of God, you may feel inadequate to deal with pressing issues or feel that you lack the ability to bring to pass God's will in your life.

There is a unique story in the Bible that deals with these kinds of problems. In Judges chapter seven we read of the challenge that

Gideon faced. He was called of God to deliver God's people. God told Him he would. Told him he could. God sent him.

Gideon started out with an army of 32,000 men. After the fearful went home he had 10,000. But, God said that he still had too many men. After another test, Gideon ended up with 300 men. Now, that's quite a drop from 32,000. But, the Scriptures give us the reason for this: God wanted the glory! If Gideon had enough men to win the battle, then God wouldn't get the glory. With only 300 men to fight a great army that vastly outnumbered his, if there was a victory, it would indeed be a miracle. And a miracle it was! God used Gideon and his 300 men to bring about a great victory for the Israelites that day.

Here is the message that we need to hear. **Whatever you have left is enough to fulfill God's plan for your life!** When life has subtracted when you thought it should be adding; when circumstances say that you will never fulfill your dream; when hard times take away your vision and your sight is blurred with tears of pain and hurt; when you know what you could've been, but can't quite arrive, remember what God showed Gideon and the Israelites. Whatever you end up with will be enough to see God's will performed in your life. You may be someone whose faith has been waylaid. Someone whose belief system has been attacked. Someone whose fear has overwhelmed them. Someone who's just not sure if God's Word is still true. God knows and God understands. If you can muster enough strength to come back into His presence with a broken heart and a humbled spirit in heartfelt repentance, what you have left is what God will use to bring you through to victory! That is a promise from the Word of God.

Zechariah 4:6, *"Not by might, nor by power, but by my spirit, saith the LORD of hosts."*

2 Corinthians 12:10, *"Therefore I take pleasure in infirmities, in reproaches, in necessities, in persecutions, in distresses for Christ's sake: for when I am weak, then am I strong."*

Bring your weakness to God. Present it to Him and allow God's will to be performed in your life through His strength. I believe that God receives glory when we, as weak humans, in all of our mistakes and failures, keep trying and keep praying and keep trusting God.

There may be some who need a sign from God. I personally believe that if your faith is rooted in a perfect or complete love of God, you don't need a sign to keep going if the Word from God is sure and known. But, if you do need a sign, just ask. Gideon asked not once, but twice! His faith was weak. But, God answered with the fleece. So, yes, you can ask for a sign and God will give it.

Why? Because God is not through with you yet. **And, what you have left is enough to bring to pass the will of God in your life.**

Have Ye Received the Holy Ghost Since Ye Believed
Part 1

The Holy Ghost has prompted me to ask you the same question that the Apostle Paul asked a group of believers at Ephesus. The question that he asked the 12 men was, *"Have ye received the Holy Ghost since ye believed?"*(Acts 19:2). I want you to answer that question today.

If you believe in the Lord Jesus Christ, in His death, burial and resurrection, have you received the Holy Ghost since then?

Some may respond, "I think so". Others, "I guess so". Others may say, "The preacher said I did", while others will have no doubt. Those without a doubt must base their experience upon the Word of God.

Some believe that in the act of believing, they received the Spirit. That, of course, is based upon an assumption. They believe that they received the Holy Spirit at the point of believing, since the Scripture says, *"Know ye not that ye are the temple of God, and that the Spirit of God dwelleth in you?"* (I Corinthians 3:16). So, some assume that when they believed, they were automatically filled with the Spirit.

Notice Romans 8:9, *"But ye are not in the flesh, but in the Spirit, if so be that the Spirit of God dwell in you. Now if any man have not the Spirit of Christ, he is none of his."*

IF SO BE that the Spirit of God dwell in you; this is written to believers. You need to remember that the New Testament epistles were written to believers. The birth of the church is recorded in the book of Acts as we see the gospel preached and new believers added to the church. The epistles are written to believers who have already been told to repent of their sins, to be baptized in the name of Jesus Christ for the remission of their sins, and that they shall receive the gift of the Holy Ghost (Acts 2:38).

Scripture plainly states that receiving the baptism of the Holy Ghost is a separate work of grace in a believer's walk with God. Scripture plainly reveals (by the early church experience) that receiving the Holy Ghost is a subsequent act after repentance of sins (See Acts 8:14-16; Acts 19:1-6).

For the past couple of weeks I have been teaching on the subject of sound doctrine at the Wednesday night Bible study. Doctrinal teaching is a necessity for a person to experience the spiritual growth that they need in their walk with God. **Doctrine is simply what you believe.** Sound doctrine is what the Bible teaches. Doctrine is needed.

I spoke to a man in San Antonio, Texas a few years ago and asked him what his church taught on the subject of being born again. After telling me that he had been a member of this church for over 20 years, he told me that he didn't know what the pastor believed about being saved. He guessed that you just believed. That's sad that he didn't know what his pastor or church believed about Christian conversion after attending services for 20 years!

Sound doctrine is necessary to rightly divide the Word of God and to convince people of what you believe. Sound doctrine is needed when you are confronted with false teachers. **Sound doctrine will always be in line with all of the Word of God.** Too many people take philosophy and try to match Scriptures to their man-made thinking. **It's sound doctrine to take the Scripture and match your thinking to it!**

Too many today take a portion of the Word of God then leave out, or disregard what is uncomfortable or inconvenient for them, thereby destroying sound doctrine.

It is quite obvious that if you take the question that Paul asked the Ephesians, you have to acknowledge that believing and being Spirit filled are two different things.

I find the writing in the People's New Testament Commentary to be interesting. "This gift disappeared at an early date from the church". The writer of this commentary has to admit that the infilling of the Holy Ghost with the evidence of speaking in tongues was received and practiced in the first church. Please show me when it stopped, scripturally. You can't. You can take I Corinthians chapter 13 and twist its meaning all to pieces, but it still doesn't say that spiritual gifts ceased with the death of the Apostles. It just doesn't say it. And, furthermore to say that this gift of the Holy Spirit ceased at an early date is inconsistent with millions of those who have received it.

I received the baptism of the Holy Ghost and found myself speaking in a language that I did not understand, and that I could not speak, outside of the Spirit. This was after I was raised in a denominational church that told me that this experience wasn't for me. One day it happened to me! Don't tell me that that gift disappeared at an early date from the church. Folks, it's still happening. Furthermore, not only did I receive the Holy Ghost some 36 years ago, but I still talk in tongues on a daily basis. It's an important part of my relationship with God. It's God speaking through me. It has created a personal relationship with God that I never came close to having before receiving this gift from God. The gift of the Holy Ghost!

When Nicodemus came to Jesus in St. John 3, the Lord told him that he needed to be born again of the water and of the Spirit. The water corresponds with being baptized for the remission of sins and the Spirit corresponds with the gift of the Holy Ghost being received as on the day of Pentecost in Acts chapter 2 (See Acts 2:38).

The Apostle Paul came to Ephesus and found twelve men who were believers in Jesus Christ but without the Spirit. How did he know they didn't have the Holy Ghost? Something triggered this question. Perhaps he just discerned it in through the Spirit. On the other hand, a person with the Holy Ghost baptism and a person without it are very different. Generally, you don't have to be around someone very long before you can tell if they have the Holy Ghost or not. There's a difference in their spirit, in their attitude, and in their faith. It's sometimes hard to explain, but when God is dwelling in a person, you know it! The Spirit bears witness!

Have you received the Holy Ghost since you believed?

Have Ye Received the Holy Ghost Since Ye Believed
Part 2

We know that Christ came to forgive us our sins. John 3:16-17, *"For God so loved the world, that he gave his only begotten Son, that whosoever believeth in him should not perish, but have everlasting life. For God sent not his Son into the world to condemn the world; but that the world through him might be saved."*

Thank God for the blood. Christianity without the shedding of blood is not Biblical. Hebrews 9:22, *"And almost all things are by the law purged with blood; and without shedding of blood is no remission."* I thank God for His sacrifice. Jesus Christ was God incarnate, God manifest in the flesh.

Still that is not the end of the story of redemption. The sad part of the Jewish religious ordinances, rituals, and history was the fact that as a type of salvation to come, the Old Testament tabernacle plan was only a shadow of God's perfect plan to come. Even with his sins forgiven, man still went out and sinned again, and again, and again. An innocent animal had to give his life to cover the sins of man, which in reality could never forgive sin.

Hebrews 10:1-4 says, *"For the law having a shadow of good things to come, and not the very image of the things, can never with those sacrifices which they offered year by year continually make the comers thereunto perfect. For then would they not have ceased to be offered? Because that the worshippers once purged should have had no more conscience of sins. But in those sacrifices there is a remembrance again made of sins every year. For it is not possible that the blood of bulls and of goats should take away sins."*

God had promised by prophets in the Old Testament and by Jesus Christ's own preaching, that someday God would take out the stony heart of man that tended to ungodliness. He would replace it with a heart of flesh that would love to do the laws of God.

"For this is the covenant that I will make with the house of Israel after those days, saith the Lord; I will put my laws into their mind, and write them in their hearts: and I will be to them a God, and they shall be to me a people" (Hebrews 8:10).

There are many other Scriptures that teach this same truth.

For example, Jesus said in John 7:38-39, *"He that believeth on me, as the scripture hath said, out of his belly shall flow rivers of living water. (But this spake he of the Spirit, which they that believe on him should receive: for the Holy Ghost was not yet given; because that Jesus was not yet glorified.)"*

This promise of God in us was fulfilled on the Day of Pentecost when the Spirit fell on 120 believers in the upper room.

Not only were our sins forgiven through the redemption at Calvary, but the way was made and the opportunity was given for believers to be filled with the Spirit. This infilling enabled them to live in the world but not be of the world. Jesus called it being "born again" (John 3:7). We were born, dead in our trespasses and sins. Outside of an intervention from God, there was no hope of ever overcoming this inbred tendency to sin. *"As it is written, There is none righteous, no, not one"* (Romans 3:10).

This is why Jesus told Nicodemus that he couldn't see or enter into the Kingdom of God unless he was born again of the water and the Spirit. Don't allow yourself to be deceived in thinking that you can get to heaven without being born again the Bible way.

Why do you think there are dead, dull, dry, lifeless churches in the land today? Is it not because the congregation has never been taught that they need to receive the Spirit into their lives? Most have been told that it was an automatic happening; that they wouldn't feel anything; there wouldn't be a big change in their life; they were just to believe that they had received it.

But, the question is still the same that the great Apostle Paul asked those men at Ephesus. **Have you received the Holy Ghost since you believed?**

This infilling of the Holy Ghost is available to every sincere seeker of God. In fact, it may just be the missing link between what you thought you would feel when you got saved, and what you actually felt! There is power in being filled with the Holy Ghost! You'll know it. You'll feel it. Everybody around you will know it! Your friends will see it. Your family will surely notice it! There's nothing to compare with being Spirit-filled!

Have Ye Received the Holy Ghost Since Ye Believed
Part 3

My first recollection of Pentecostals was when I was a child, perhaps 10 or 11 years old. My parents, my two brothers and I had gone to Muncie, Indiana, which was the nearest big town to our small community. While driving we came across a large tent where a Pentecostal revival service was in progress. Dad parked in the grass close enough where we could get a glimpse inside and hear the music. My only real memory that evening was that I enjoyed the music and noticed the people were certainly having a good time.

When I was 15 I started a singing group. I was probably about 17 or 18 when we were invited to sing at a trinity Pentecostal church. I had sung in nearly every other evangelical denomination around our part of the country, but never in a Pentecostal church, so I was looking forward to going. Our trio sang. I don't recall anything particularly outstanding about the service. It actually wasn't too different from what I was used to. But, afterwards a man came up to me, very friendly, very kind, and asked me a question that bugged me for several years. He asked, "Have you received the baptism of the Holy Ghost?"

I had been around enough to know that what he meant was had I spoken in tongues as evidence of the infilling of the Holy Ghost. On the other hand, I had been taught that you didn't have to do that. I was taught that I already had it. I didn't know what to say. My answer to him needed to be "no". I knew what he meant. At the same time, my pride stopped me, and I stuttered something about I think so and tried to turn away from him.

What the man never knew was what was going on inside of me. Although totally accepted by my church denomination, I absolutely knew there was something missing in my walk with God. My singing group was accepted. I had been the church organist since the age of 13. No one openly doubted my walk with God. I had been to the altar twice. I had been saved and sanctified by their standards. I testified to the same. But, I knew there was something missing. So, when that man asked me if I had received the Holy Ghost, I was very aware that he had sensed there was something missing in my walk with God.

At that time I didn't understand how he knew. But he did. Even to this day, some 40 years later, I can still remember the blush, the embarrassment, the frustration. No, I didn't have the Holy Ghost, and although I didn't admit it to him at the time, I never forgot that encounter with a soul that cared enough for me to ask me a most important question; actually a Biblical question. The same question that the Apostle Paul asked the Ephesians in Acts 19:2 when *"He said unto them, Have ye received the Holy Ghost since ye believed?"* My answer could have truthfully been the same as theirs: *"We have not so much as heard whether there be any Holy Ghost."*

Paul's next question was this: *"Unto what then were ye baptized?"* If I had been asked that question I would have had to answer that I had not been baptized. In our church we had water baptisms by immersion about once a year down on the river bank in our town, actually right on the golf course. It was a beautiful setting. My pastor had asked me 2 or 3 times about getting baptized and I had always rejected baptism. I knew I wasn't right with God. I knew there was something missing in my life. I needed something in my experience that I didn't have. What was missing was the Holy Ghost!

The Holy Ghost baptism changes everything! Receiving the Holy Ghost completes your new birth. It brings you into the Body of Christ through the Spirit! If you don't know that you have it, you don't! **You will KNOW when you have been baptized in the Holy Ghost!**

You can repent of your sins, which you must do. The preacher can baptize you in water in the name of our Lord Jesus Christ, which is for the remission of your sins (See Acts 2:38). But, only God can fill you with the Holy Ghost! You can't fake it. You can't buy it. You can't make it happen. All you can do is yield to the Spirit of God by separating yourself from the world and giving up every sin and weight that doth so easily beset you. When you yield yourself to the power of God, surrendering your own life to the will of God, I promise you, based upon the never changing Word of God, that God can and will fill you with the baptism of the Holy Ghost!

These twelve men in Acts chapter 19 believed on the Lord, and to so many today, that is more than enough. However, to the early church, that was not enough. Paul knew they needed the power of God within them! He knew they needed what he had! What the 120 had received on the day of Pentecost was evidenced by speaking in other tongues as the Spirit gave utterance.

Look at what happened to the household of Cornelius. Acts 10:44-46, says that *"While Peter yet spake these words, the Holy Ghost fell on all them which heard the word. And they of the circumcision which believed were astonished, as many as came with Peter, because that on the Gentiles also was poured out the gift of the Holy Ghost. **For they heard them speak with tongues, and magnify God."***

Peter later rehearsed the matter to the church at Jerusalem with these words: Acts 11:15-17, *"And as I began to speak, the Holy Ghost fell on them, as on us at the beginning. Then remembered I the word of the Lord, how that he said, John indeed baptized with water; but ye shall be baptized with the Holy Ghost. Forasmuch then as God gave them the like gift as he did unto us, who believed on the Lord Jesus Christ;"*

Just like the Ephesians, the common experience of those who received the Holy Ghost in the book of Acts was the initial evidence of speaking in other tongues as the Spirit gave the utterance.

Have you received the Holy Ghost since you believed?

Hope

I was speaking recently with a young person who was suicidal. He had suffered several losses including his job and a relationship and was having to move to another part of the state. Hope was gone.

Problem after problem can create a very real feeling of hopelessness. A person without hope has no reason for living. The old devil's going to come around with suicidal thoughts as the only way out of this dilemma. While the mind says it is a dilemma, in reality it is an opportunity if God is placed in the equation. God is a way maker. God is a provider. God is a healer. God is a present-day miracle worker.

Without God, these things are impossible. **With God all things are possible.** This whole premise is based upon the fact of Christ's resurrection. Notice, I said fact. It's not a theory. It's not a fairy tale. It's not a parable. It's not a theology of some off-the-wall religious kook. It's a fact.

The resurrection of Christ is a proven fact by the large number of witnesses, by the written accounts, and by the lives of millions of believers over the last 2000 years who have experienced the living Savior in their own lives. To us, it is a fact that Jesus Christ did not stay in the borrowed tomb. He came out alive on Easter Sunday morning, and He's still alive today.

I Peter 1:3, *"Blessed be the God and Father of our Lord Jesus Christ, which according to his abundant mercy hath begotten us again unto a lively hope by the resurrection of Jesus Christ from the dead."*

By the resurrection of Jesus Christ, we have a lively hope—a living hope. When He conquered death, He changed the whole landscape of religions. No other religion in the world, then or now, has a founder who died and three days later came back to life and ascended to Heaven! I like the fact that although there are those in America who don't want the Christian faith to be public, this Easter weekend is all about one thing: Easter! Resurrection! Alive! It's all about our Lord and Savior Jesus Christ. I do find it appalling that America has come to the place that when a public person or a media personality mentions Easter, they feel obligated to apologize to other religions. Apologize for what? We're living in a Christian America. Our biggest holidays are Christian holidays. You can't change the fact that both are based upon the Christian faith. Even Thanksgiving is a time of giving thanks to God, recognizing that there is a higher power, a God that we thank for our blessings. I do not apologize for mentioning Easter. Everyone needs to hear the truth. He lives!

Matthew 27: 64-66, *"Command therefore that the sepulchre be made sure until the third day, lest his disciples come by night, and steal him away, and say unto the people, He is risen from the dead: so the last error shall be worse than the first. Pilate said unto them, Ye have a watch: go your way, make it as sure as ye can. So they went, and made the sepulchre sure, sealing the stone, and setting a watch."*

I love the humor of God. Just to make sure that it was official and that everyone knew that Jesus was in that tomb, Pilate, in securing the sepulchre with a seal and providing several soldiers to guard it, took away any possibility that His resurrection could have been faked or staged by His disciples. God must have snickered at least a little. Pilate provided the security that would make the resurrection an obvious miracle.

You may be in a situation that you would compare to a grave. And not only are you down and out, but it feels like Satan has put a guard at your door so you can't get out even if you were able. It may be drug addiction, alcoholism, a homosexual lifestyle, bondage of witchcraft or feelings of hopelessness. Jesus can still get you out! He came out of the grave. You can get out, too! It's not impossible. It's just a situation that God can turn around in a moment.

You may be trapped in an abusive lifestyle.

Your body may be trapped in physical ailments that have destroyed your hope.

Your mind may be buried in years of bad thinking and hopelessness.

But, because He lives, you can live too. That's why the gospel is so rewarding to preach. Lives are changed. I'm not wasting my time by telling you about the resurrection of Jesus Christ. I'm sharing life-changing words and thoughts that can turn your life around if you'll turn your life over to Jesus Christ.

In the Scriptures, the chief priests and Pharisees remembered that Jesus had said He would come out of the grave after three days. But, evidently, His followers didn't remember, or at least didn't believe it as much as those religious leaders did. If so, there would have been a crowd of people at the tomb on Easter Sunday waiting for His promised resurrection. But, there was no one there.

 I would like to think that I would have been the one that would have had the faith and would've camped out all night, ready for this unbelievable miracle to take place.

But, being realistic, I suppose I would have been like the others, and missed a great opportunity to see something that has only happened to a handful of people. And, the widow's son and Lazarus had to die again. But, not Jesus! He's still alive!

Notice in Matthew 27:64 that the religious leaders were worried that if someone thought there was a resurrection, that mistake would be worse than the first mistake. They were saying that it is bad enough that some think He's the Messiah. Let's not give them any reason to believe that He came back from the dead. And, yet, through their actions, we have absolute proof that He's alive.

The devil is sly; he's like a roaring lion, roaming to and fro through the earth, and he's a deceiver. But, he sure makes a lot of mistakes in his determination to usurp the authority of God. He always goes too far.

He buries you so far that you realize that God is your only hope!

And, when you come to the end of your rope, you will find God there. When you fall down in life, you will fall into the hands of the Lord.

When you come to your wits end, you will find God there.

He's the rock at the bottom of the pit that you find yourself in today.

There is hope. His name is Jesus. Christianity is not a meditation plan, nor a philosophy for discussion; it's not a mind exercise in positive thinking. It's experiencing the power of a living Savior through being born again of the water and the Spirit.

Unstoppable

A recent article in Charisma Magazine stated that preachers need to quit preaching negative sermons and that Christians should just live out their lives in positive love. The author was referring to what he sees as the negative slant of preaching the gospel, which by its nature, requires repentance. Obviously, for a person to repent, they must recognize their sin. So, a person needs to hear about their sins, which is negative. So, he recommended preaching a more uplifting "social gospel."

But what this author was referring to does not produce Christians; it produces church members. A social gospel doesn't give birth to Christians, just believers. Believers who don't recognize sin when they see it! And, sin will be judged. Whether you acknowledge sin or not, you will be judged for your disobedience to God's Word.

During recent camp meeting services in Nashville, Tennessee, Bro. Raymond Woodward of Fredericton, NB, Canada, taught on the subject of how the gospel is unstoppable. He used the last words of the book of Acts, as recorded in chapter 28, verses 30-31, "*And Paul dwelt two whole years in his own hired house, and received all that came in unto him, preaching the kingdom of God, and teaching those things which concern the Lord Jesus Christ, with all confidence, no man forbidding him*".

The book of Acts has no ending; it doesn't actually end at all. We are still making entries into that book! That last phrase, **No man forbidding him** is actually one word: "Akolutos" which in the Greek means, "unhindered or freely". Literally unstoppable.

The Apostle Paul was under house arrest and not a free man. But, as he preached the Lord Jesus Christ, with all confidence, he was unstoppable! How was this possible? **Paul was not ashamed of the gospel and knew that it was the power of God!** (Romans 1:16). The power of God unto salvation for every living soul. So, he was simply unstoppable. No man could hinder him.

I'm afraid that if we were in his shoes, we would have been stoppable! How many can keep the faith and keep preaching even in the face of adversity? I can tell you, not many. We know that Paul wrote Ephesians, II Timothy, Philippians, Colossians, Philemon and Hebrews from jail cells! He had confidence in the power of God. Sometimes God shakes the prison and sets us free. Other times, we have to face adversity. But, either way, we are unstoppable if we can keep our faith and trust in God!

The tactic of the enemy today is to teach us learned helplessness.

To make us think we are helpless to overcome the present trial.

Learned helplessness tells us that we can't overcome harmful habits. Learned helplessness says, I've failed before…I'll fail again. And, because we've not overcome a problem before, we can't this time, either.

A Christian is not helpless! We are never without hope! Paul wrote, from prison, *"I can do all things through Christ which strengthenth me!"* (Philippians 4:13).

The impotent man at the pool of Bethesda was helpless to get into the pool in time for his healing. But one day Jesus Christ showed up. Now, all he had to do was to rise, take up his bed and walk. The gospel is unstoppable!

The gospel is not weak. It is only weak if it is watered down! It is only weak if someone tries to make it easier to digest. It's only weak when people don't want to hear the truth! When people have itching ears to hear only what they want to hear.

In author Mark Labberton's book, the *Dangerous Act of Worship* he writes: "The God we seek is the God we want; not the God who is. We fashion a God who blesses without obligation, who lets us feel His presence without living IIis life, Who stands with us and never against us, Who gives us what we want, when we want it" (Labberton).

God help us to get a hold of the gospel of Jesus Christ. The death, burial and resurrection preached will still change people's lives when they repent of their sins, and are water baptized in the name of Jesus Christ for the remission of their sins and they receive the gift of the Holy Ghost! (See Acts 2:38; 8:14-17; 10:44-48; 19:1-6).

That is unstoppable!

What Happened to the Fear of the Lord

I come from a generation that knew at least a reasonable fear of the Lord. My generation was taught respect for our parents; respect for our elders; respect for our school teachers, policemen, figures of authority, and especially respect for the preacher and the house of the Lord. Somehow in the last 40 years, things have changed. America is not the same America that I grew up in. Respect is realized as missing, but no one dares teach it because that would impose upon individual freedoms. Is that gross ignorance or what? What happened to common sense in America?

Many laws in America fly in the face of common sense. I read this week where someone is going to sue a school teacher because their unruly child was corrected in a manner that they didn't like. I'm not saying whether the correction was right or wrong. All I know is, if I got corrected at school, my mom and dad would have supported the teacher 100%, and thereby instilled in me respect for my school teachers. I think you know what I'm trying to say.

The lack of respect that I'm concerned about is the lack of a fear of the Lord. In Matthew 3:11 we read, *"I indeed baptize you with water unto repentance: but he that cometh after me is mightier than I, whose shoes I am not worthy to bear: he shall baptize you with the Holy Ghost, and with fire:"*

Fire is a cleansing flame that burns up sin and produces the fear of the Lord. The baptism of the Holy Ghost, as the early church received it, brought spiritual power, but we fail to emphasize that it also brought Holy Ghost fire. Not just enthusiasm, but a cleansing fire. When the bodies of Ananias and Sapphira were carried away after dropping dead because they lied to the Holy Ghost, the Bible says the great fear came over the whole church. This fear was not just a reverence, but the word also refers to exceeding dread, alarm or terror.

That kind of fear would bring a revival of Biblical proportions to our land. I'm not praying for people to drop dead in the church. I'm not praying for tragedies to fall upon church members. But, I am praying for a godly fear to grip our hearts. I believe that this kind of fear is missing and desperately needed in the church today. This lack of fear is demonstrated in the casual attitude that people have toward church, and thereby God today.

First of all, very few people will go to church today expecting a God encounter. A person should! But, most don't. In fact, most don't even know what I'm talking about: a God encounter and a realization that God is in the place—a manifested presence of God that will be felt. Worship that is heartfelt. Preaching that is anointed from heaven. Not just a well-structured talk, speech or exhortation, but a sermon delivered with the passion of a man of God that has been in the presence of God and has been sent to deliver his soul to the congregation. A God encounter, where tears flow, where sinners willingly repent, where new converts are baptized in the name of Jesus Christ for the remission of their sins and where believers are filled with the Holy Ghost, speaking in other tongues as the Spirit gives the utterance. Where the sick are healed and the discouraged find a Word from the Lord. A God encounter!

Because none of this is expected, then just come as you are. Come casual. Don't worry about putting on your "Sunday best". That's what I had as a kid. I had play clothes, school clothes, and then I had church clothes. By that, I don't mean they were expensive or fancy. I just knew that my best clothes were for church. The casual approach to God is so anti-Biblical that it is amazing to me that so many people are taken in by it.

In the Word of God people always prepared for their encounter with God. The Old Testament is often used in types and shadows of the New Testament church. When people came into the presence of the Lord they came prepared: sanctified, separated from the world. They were clean. How much more today, when the Spirit of the Lord lives with us, and we are the temple of God?

In too many modern-day churches you know you are going to hear feel-good oratory about how to live a better life and get more things to park in your garage and have better health by eating better. Perhaps a sermon about reaching out to others who are not as fortunate as you are, but not a God encounter. It just won't happen. Why? Because the casual approach to God is a dead give away to what is in the heart of man.

Do you fear God? Do you respect your pastor as a "man of God?" Or would you confront him on any day on any nit-picking thing that you disagreed with him about?

There are obvious, glaring reasons why revival tarries, the church slumbers, and our families and neighbors go to hell.

Revival must not tarry any longer! We need a Holy Ghost revival today. But, if that is to happen, there is going to have to be big changes made in the way that people act, in the way they feel about God and their level of fear of the Lord.

Understanding God's Purpose

Life is not easy. The truth is life can be very difficult, even for a Christian with strong faith. But, it is the devil's business to try and steal your faith, to destroy your confidence in the Bible and Christian leaders, and to leave you without an anchor on life's troubled sea.

I know how it feels to wonder if my faith in God is just a fairy tale. I've been battered in times past by questions like, "maybe this Christian stuff is just a psychological cop-out. Really now, if God is really real, why am I suffering like this? Why did this problem happen to me?" I can remember one season in my life, many years ago now, when my mind was bombarded with such thoughts. It's not that I wanted to think negative about my faith, my spiritual experiences, or my ministry, but the thoughts were there, literally for months. Our family ministry was going through changes and times were tough. And, I felt that God ought to be doing more than He was doing. I felt that I had given years to His service and it looked like it was time for payback from God. But, answers were not coming. Problems were not being solved. Finances were not being supplied. It drove me to my knees in prayer and fasting.

During this time of seeking God, the devil was working overtime to try to get me to give up. Thoughts were going through my mind like "Maybe all this talk and preaching about faith was man's way of coping with problems. Maybe Scriptures that I preached from about faith and miracles were being taken out of context. Perhaps God isn't going to intervene. Maybe He is just going to let me down."

In the midst of a particularly bad day, I went upstairs to my study and cried out to God. I said, "God, if this ship goes down, You're going down with me because I am not going to let go of You!" I meant it. From the bottom of my heart I meant it. I was desperate for something from God. The very next day God wrought a miracle in my life that was a sure sign to me that He had heard my prayer. That experience became a turning point in my life and preaching ministry. It was something that I could point to—a monument—a specific time and place when it happened. And, life went on, even though Satan had told me it wouldn't...it did. Our ministry went on and God did make a way!

Today, some 25 years later, I look back on that experience and realize that God was trying to increase my faith by delaying an answer until I came into an understanding that God was real. He cared. He answered prayer. He was a miracle worker. **Regardless of what the problem was, I learned to trust God.**

Notice the Scripture in John 11:32, *"Then when Mary was come where Jesus was, and saw him, she fell down at his feet, saying unto him, Lord, if thou hadst been here, my brother had not died."*

Mary was saying, "Lord, if you would've come when we called, my brother would not have died. God, you failed me. You could have prevented this from happening."

Listen now to what pastor and author Henry Blackaby writes in the book *Experiencing God*. (He writes this as a response that God might have given to Mary).

> "You are exactly right. If I had come, your brother would not have died. You know that I could have healed him, because you have seen me heal many, many times. If I had come when you asked me to, I would have healed him. But, you would have never known any more about Me than you already know. I knew that you were ready for a greater revelation of Me than you have ever

known in your life. I wanted you to come to know that I am the resurrection and the life. My refusal and My silence was not rejection. It was an opportunity for Me to disclose to you more of Me than you have ever known."

Blackaby

Can you see that when we whine, complain, cry, and sometimes even quit our faith, that we are hindering what God is trying to reveal to us? I've seen people who will live for God when things are going well, but as soon as a trial comes their way, out the door they go. They'll give up on living for God, go out into a sinful lifestyle and actually feel that God has failed them. God has never failed anyone. God has never failed to come through for anyone who will dare trust Him completely. So, when a person walks out on God while going through a trial, they flunk that test. They fail to learn what God was trying to show them, and in reality, fail to see God in a fresh, new, powerful way in their life.

How about you? If you were Mary would you have said the same thing to Jesus? She was actually scolding Him.

Isaiah 59:1, *"Behold, the LORD'S hand is not shortened, that it cannot save; neither his ear heavy, that it cannot hear: 2 But your iniquities have separated between you and your God, and your sins have hid his face from you, that he will not hear."*

The first thing you need to do is to repent of your unbelief. You won't get anywhere until you see that you were the one that failed. Repent. Tell God you're sorry for your failure to trust Him through this situation you're going through. Once you've repented, you can pick up the pieces, and start over, and you will see the Lord come through again. He always has, He always will. Remember, His promises are all conditional. Obey His commandments. He will take care of you! Learn of Him anew. **Let Him show you what He can do through someone who will totally trust Him.**

The Worst Thing is Not the Last Thing—Part 1

I was reading in a devotional one day when this line jumped out at me. **"The worst thing is not the last thing."**

That phrase has changed my life and continues to give me hope when despair tries to come in.

Some are facing life with small chance of survival. Old age has brought fear to some. Financial problems have brought despair to families. Divorce has brought anger and uncertainty to others. A loss of a job has brought insecurity to some. Sickness has brought a loss of hope to a loved one.

But, God is still on the throne and God's Word still has the answer. I encourage you to lift up your head, lift up your heart and see your problems in a way you have never seen them before.

Let me start here. In Mark chapter 4, Jesus was asleep on a ship while a storm was beating it to death and the disciples thought they were going to die. They had to wake Jesus up. Don't ever get the idea that if God wants you to have healing, deliverance or salvation, that He'll just give it to you. No! The Bible makes it plain that if you want something from God, you ask and then receive. Seek then you will find. Knock and it shall be opened. Some people are going to hell because they've never sought God. Some are sick because they've never prayed for healing. Oh, they would like to be saved or healed. But, it's just up to God. No, it's up to you! It's time to get to the house of God, get to praying and fasting and see what God will do for you!

Now, when Jesus woke up, He calmed the water with the words "Peace, be still". Think of the raw power of God's Word! Then He asked the disciples a question. He didn't ask how the boat was. He didn't ask if the sails were intact. He didn't ask if anyone was seasick after the rough ride. He asked, "Why are ye so fearful. How is it that ye have no faith?" He asked about their faith! He wanted to know if their faith was still intact.

Storms come into your life not to destroy *you*, but to destroy your faith. While we think we're dying, our faith is actually what is being attacked. **Satan can't take your life.**

And, I know that some at this moment are experiencing things in your life that are the worst they could possibly be. **But, this storm in your life is not going to destroy you. It came to destroy your faith**. God is interested in how your faith is holding out. God is concerned that while other things in your life are being destroyed, that you don't lose your faith in His Word! Things are things. They can be replaced. Life will go on.

That's the bad part for some. Perhaps you are one of those who really don't want life to go on. You just want a change in your life so bad. You're weary of the path you have to walk in. And perhaps the worst thing possible is getting ready to take place. Maybe I'm talking about a job loss, a bankruptcy, a divorce, or a life threatening disease. The worst possible thing is getting ready to happen to you. Be of good courage. I am telling you that the worst thing is not the last thing!

While Satan has been trying to sink your faith, you just need to know that **after the worst thing in your life has happened, you're still going to go on, and the worst thing is not the last thing.**

I meet people nearly every week who have faced the worst thing in their life, and now some years later, they discovered they lived on, but what was destroyed was not what they thought would be destroyed. In reality they lost their faith! Today they no longer enjoy worshiping with their friends at church. Many are involved in activities and habits that are not Christ-like. They have let their lives get out of control to the point that their backslidden state is much worse than what they thought was going to happen to them when they faced the worst thing some time ago.

You see, Satan convinces us that God doesn't care and isn't concerned about our well-being. And, generally it is other people that get between us and God. If you've fallen away from the place you once knew in Christ, it was probably people that got in your way. **Keep your eyes on Jesus, not people, and everything will be alright!**

Don't quit church when you're going through a trial. Don't quit on God when your faith is tested. Don't get bitter at the ministry when things aren't working out for you. Don't get your eyes on people when the storms of life start blowing and your boat is rocking. That's the time to head to the house of God. Pray like you've never prayed. Worship like you've never worshiped. Sing like you've never sung before. Give like you've never given before. Love like you've never loved before.

Remember the three Hebrew children? They were in a strange land with strange customs and were being made to worship a strange god. That's bad. But, if that wasn't bad enough, if they didn't worship that idol of that strange god, they were going to be burnt alive. That's really bad.

Let's face it. That's about the worst thing that could happen to someone. Things couldn't get much worse than that. The date was set and they were given another opportunity to deny their faith. But, they were resolute believing that their God was the only God, and there was no room for compromise. There was no room for an idol god. If it cost them their life, they weren't going to deny their God.

They found out what I'm trying to tell you. The worst thing was not the last thing! Being thrown into the fiery furnace was not the last chapter of their life! **And, what you're facing today isn't the last chapter in your life**. The worst thing is not the last thing.

The Worst Thing is Not the Last Thing—Part 2

Knowing that without faith it is impossible to please God, it is imperative that you understand that Satan is out to destroy your faith. Satan's arena of battle is in your mind. The disabling of your faith enables doubt, fear, unbelief and all kinds of other evil spirits to get control of your thought life thereby destroying your strength in God's Word, which is the foundation of your faith.

Whatever battle you're going through today, the purpose and ultimate goal of Satan is to get you to lose your faith in God, in the church, in people, in the Bible. Whenever you get your eyes on people instead of God; whenever you get your eyes on problems instead of the problem-solver...you're in trouble. Your faith will waver and your prayers will not be answered: you actually hinder God from doing what He would do in your life. **Without faith it is impossible to please Him.**

The worst thing is not the last thing.

The worst thing possible could be facing you. Perhaps it's tomorrow morning when you must face a lawyer, banker, preacher, spouse, or your children and you expect the worst thing in your life to happen to you. Perhaps it's already happened and you're reeling from the emotional fallout of a failure, a bad judgment, disease or just a twist of fate that has your life upside down and confused about the future.

Well, I'm here to tell you, that according to the Word of God, the worst thing is not the last thing. If you are a child of God, a born-again Christian, you can be assured that God will get the last word! If you're not saved, but seeking after God, let me assure you that God loves you and wants to work that miracle you need in your life. Please know that God uses trials and sicknesses to get your attention. That doesn't mean that He put the problem or disease into your life, but He will use the occasion to get you on your knees and to re-adjust your thinking and put God back into your life where He belongs.

The three Hebrew children were facing the worst possible experience in life. They were about to be thrown into the fiery furnace for their faith. But, when they arrived, they were met by a fourth man in the fire. Isn't that beautiful! I've had that same experience. No, not a real fiery furnace, but I think I felt the same as they did. **In life, we don't all walk down the same road, but we do have the same feelings**. We don't have the same trials, but we have the same doubts and fears. Thank God, we can have the same faith, too!

The three Hebrew children discovered what I'm preaching to you today. **The worst thing was not the last thing**. God had other plans! Life went on! God received glory!

Daniel discovered the same thing in the lion's den. You may be literally disabled by your mind's torment, but listen to what I'm saying. You've thought the worst was going to happen, and when it happened, you discovered you're still here. Look at Daniel. I would venture to say that, that was the worst possible thing that could happen to him that day. **But, it wasn't the last thing!** God put the clamps on those lion's mouths and Daniel lived to tell the story.

Romans 8:28, *"And we know that all things work together for good to them that love God, to them who are the called according to his purpose."* **Our idea of victory is to be kept from the problem.** God, why me? What have I done to deserve this kind of problem? Why do I have to suffer through these medical treatments?

If we're not careful, we can get bitter towards God, or people, and get deeper in doubt and unbelief.

I want to clarify something for someone today. You don't have to be beaten down by your problems. Of course there are natural recourses that have to be worked through. Relationships, emotions, even finances have to be taken care of. But, remember, the worst thing is not the last thing! How many times have you dreaded a confrontation, and then to your amazement you soon realized that **confronting that problem was the best thing that could have happened to you**.

I could give you example after example in the Scripture. Peter's denial of Jesus Christ was bad. But, it wasn't final. He survived to preach on the day of Pentecost.

The storm that came upon the disciples in the middle of the night, in the middle of the sea, was the worst thing and they feared for their life. But, it wasn't the last thing. Jesus came walking on the water.

The woman at the well had experienced life at its worst. She had been married five times and was living in adultery. You think she was happy? Not hardly! You think she had all of her ducks in a row? You think life was what she had hoped for as a young teenager? No, her life had turned out as a worst case scenario. But, the worst wasn't the last. One day she met a man at the well and He told her about living water. Don't give up on your life. If you haven't met Jesus Christ yet, the best is yet to come.

How about Stephen? He was the first Christian martyr. **Even in death, the worst wasn't the last!** Acts 7:59-60 says, *"they stoned Stephen, calling upon God, and saying, Lord Jesus, receive my spirit. And he kneeled down, and cried with a loud voice, Lord, lay not this sin to their charge. And when he had said this, he fell asleep."*

The Apostle Paul said in Philippians 1:21-23 *"For to me to live is Christ, and to die is gain. For I am in a strait betwixt two, having a desire to depart, and to be with Christ; which is far better:"*

Yes, Stephen died. But, the glory which he beheld on the other side of eternity was far better than the life he lived here. So, yes, the worst possible thing in this life happened to him, but it was not the last thing. **Heaven is better than this.**

Perhaps someone today is suffering from grief over the loss of a loved one. Yes, the grief is real. Yes, the pain is real. Yes, the loss is real. But, the worst thing is not the last thing.

To the born again believer, when the worst possible thing happens to you in this life, death; it's still not over. There is a mansion just over the hilltop; streets of gold; gates of pearl; walls of jasper. Forever in the presence of our Lord and Savior, Jesus Christ. **The worst thing is not the last thing!**

The Fire Still Falls...You Just Gotta Be There

Have you ever been in an on-fire, Holy Ghost filled church service? Have you ever been so enthralled in worship that time was no longer important? Have you ever heard anointed preaching that changed your life? I trust you have.

Now, my next question is this: what would you have missed if you hadn't been there for that special service? You would have missed the manifest presence of God that comes in response to worship. You would have missed that message that changed your mind, and therefore changed your life. **Friend, the fire still falls, you just gotta be there!** Please get my point today. Jesus Christ is still the same, yesterday, today, and forever. The power of God still wants to operate in the church just like in the book of Acts. But, you've got to be where the power is falling if you are going to experience it.

Now, I'm not taking away from any personal experience. I'm not detracting from any visitation of God in any manner. **But, I wonder how many times we could've been mightily blessed, but we weren't there?** We skipped church with whatever excuse. So many people go to church only when they find it convenient. A few weeks ago someone told me as to how they had been everywhere that weekend: doctor, grocery, Walmart, family and friend's houses. But, they called to tell me they couldn't make it to church. Too sick, too tired, too worn out, so, they had taken care of all their physical and emotional needs, but were left starving spiritually. When in reality, the spiritual food was much more important than their other activities.

I hate to miss church. I hate to think what I might miss. How would God have talked to me if I had been there? What answer might I have found through the preaching of the Word? What blessing might I have obtained if I had just shown up where the fire was falling? The fire still falls. You just gotta be there!

That goes for personal prayer time, too—our personal devotion. I don't want to miss my time with the Lord. Not just because I'm a preacher and I have three sermons and a radio broadcast to prepare for this week, but also because I love the fellowship with the Lord and the blessings that come from fellowship with Him. I hear from the Lord! He speaks to me. Prayer changes things when I pray. My family is blessed when I pray for them. My needs are met when I pray. I humble myself when I pray. What would I have missed today if I had not prayed? What have you missed by not praying? What have you missed by not going to church? The fire stills falls. You just gotta be there!

God is still working miracles, answering prayers, saving souls, healing the sick just like he did here on the earth 2000 years ago. The same power is still in the church today. He said in John 14:12, *"Verily, verily, I say unto you, He that believeth on me, the works that I do shall he do also; and greater works than these shall he do; because I go unto my Father."*

In Luke 1 verse 37 we read, *"For with God nothing shall be impossible."* The Amplified Version of that verse reads: *"For with God nothing is ever impossible and no word from God shall be without power or impossible of fulfillment."*

The fire still falls! **You can't put God in an impossible situation!**

After the angel Gabriel told the Virgin Mary about bringing forth a son, the angel then told her about her cousin Elizabeth giving birth to a son in her old age. She was probably just about as shocked about Elizabeth as she was herself.

In ancient Israel, barrenness was a disgrace and looked upon as a judgment from God. But, God often used barren women to bring about His plans for mankind. He used women who had suffered reproach, not really knowing at that time that they were suffering for God's sake. God doesn't always explain everything to us humans what He is doing. That's why we learn to trust Him and, stand on His Word. Someday, we'll understand it better.

Isaac was married to a barren woman, Rebecca, but Esau and Jacob were born.

Jacob was married to a barren woman, but through prayer Joseph was born.

The mighty Samson was born of a barren woman when God needed a deliverer for His people.

Samuel was born of a barren woman when she couldn't stand being barren any longer!

And, when God was ready to send John the Baptist to prepare the way of Jesus Christ, He found a godly couple and answered their long ago prayers for a child. It's an encouragement to know that prayers that you've prayed a long time ago and have never been answered, have still been heard, and will be answered in God's time. The Bible says that the angel told Elizabeth's husband that their prayers had been heard in Luke 1:13. They hadn't been praying that prayer for many years! They wouldn't have had any reason to be praying that prayer for a child at this time in their life. But, God remembered!

Why would God use so many barren women to fulfill His ways? Could it not have been their state of humility and openness to God?

They suffered reproach in society and family. They must have cried many tears. They must have been desperate. They must have given up hope. They surely had lost their pride years before. They were mightily humbled before their God. They were available...they were there! **They were prepared for an answer to their prayers through their testing.**

I hope you can read between the lines today. These reasons are the exact reasons that God could bring His special agents into the world through these women. They were broken. They were desperate. They had given up hope in themselves. They had lost their personal ego. They were humbled before the Lord. They had an intense hunger that only a child could cure. And, they would go to their grave with that hunger. There was no other choice for them. They had to have an answer! They were there! They were prepared! Don't give up when the answer is delayed…be sure that you're not at the train station when your ship comes in!

The fire still falls. God is still the same. Keep your faith in God. He still brings His purposes to fruition. You've just gotta be there.

Prayer and Fasting—Part 1

So, what do you do when you hit a brick wall in your life? What do you do when you can't get an answer to your problem, or deliverance from an addiction? What do you do when you can't get over a hurt or you can't forgive someone who has wounded you? What do you do when your mind tells you that you will always have to suffer this way—when the enemy of your soul convinces you that you can't change the past so the future isn't worth living?

Some have struggled for years with the same nagging problem, the same ruinous habit, the same unrelenting guilt and shame. Some have even prayed and trusted God for deliverance and perhaps even been prayed for by men of God and people of faith. **But, what do you do when those walls that keep you bound just won't move?**

Ephesians 6:12 says, *"For we wrestle not against flesh and blood, but against principalities, against powers, against the rulers of the darkness of this world, against spiritual wickedness in high places."* NO, you're not crazy or stupid. You are fighting evil spirits that want to destroy your mind, your sanity, your life, your home, your family, church, finances…anything they can. You are fighting cosmic powers. One preacher said that getting answers to your prayers depends upon at least three things: **your faith, God's will and cosmic power, the rulers of the darkness of this world.**

The disciples faced such a situation early in their ministry. They faced a devil they couldn't cast out. In Matthew chapter 17, a man brought his son to the disciples and they couldn't cast the demon out of the boy. After Jesus cast him out the disciples asked the Lord why they couldn't do it.

Now, you've got to understand their situation. They HAD been casting out devils and healing the sick according to Matthew chapter 10:1, *"And when he had called unto him his twelve disciples, he gave them power against unclean spirits, to cast them out, and to heal all manner of sickness and all manner of disease."*

So, they had already experienced success at casting out unclean spirits and healing sickness and disease. But all the sudden they hit a brick wall. When they prayed and commanded this spirit to leave this boy, nothing happened; a brick wall, if you please.

You need to know where to find the answer to your brick walls, or you'll spend the rest of your life fighting the same devils, the same problems, having the same hindrances to your walk with God.

Jesus replied in Matthew 17:21, *"Howbeit this kind goeth not out but by prayer and fasting."* Prayer and fasting, almost too simple, isn't it? Prayer and fasting, we already knew, but…wow, it's hard to believe that's the answer. Isn't that what the Lord said to the disciples in verse 20, *"because of your unbelief"*? Unbelief in the power of prayer and fasting. That's what is keeping you from your victory in Jesus. **Your unbelief in the power of prayer and fasting will keep you from becoming the person that God wants you to be and from realizing the destiny that God has for you.**

Every one of us will face brick walls in our life. And, the answer is simple, but the work is sometimes hard to grasp. You must go to a new level in your spiritual life to conquer this new enemy that has attacked you. And the only scriptural way to win this battle is to pray and fast. A five minute prayer in the morning and another before bedtime won't cut it. We're talking about seeking God through prayer. Fasting involves pushing yourself away from the dinner table. It involves the body coming under subjection to the Spirit through the abstinence from food for a few meals or days. **The most powerful prayer is the request that is accompanied with fasting. Prayer and fasting moves the hand of God.**

Prayer and Fasting—Part 2

II Corinthians 10: *4-5, "(For the weapons of our warfare are not carnal, but mighty through God to the pulling down of strong holds;) Casting down imaginations, and every high thing that exalteth it-self against the knowledge of God, and bringing into captivity every thought to the obedience of Christ;"*

From this Scripture we realize that when you become a child of God, a born again Christian, you enter into warfare. You enter into a war with the devil. You're a child of God, part of the Kingdom of God, but you still live on the earth where Satan is the prince of the power of the air (See Ephesians 2:2).

Please don't be misled. Living for God is wonderful! He said, *"My yoke is easy and My burden is light"* (Matthew 11:30). But, don't think for a minute that Satan is not walking through the land seeking whom he may devour.

If you're not fighting spiritual warfare you're probably not irritating the devil. He's probably not concerned about you hindering his work. If you're not involved in battles for your soul, you're probably not a concern in the devil's camp. If you're living for God, walking in all the light you have and living a life separated from the ungodliness of this world; if you're a worshiper that is not ashamed to let the world know that you're thankful for what God has done for you, then the devil is on your trail!

In this battle there will be times when you hit a brick wall and the devil just won't move. Or, to put it a little more clearly, **there will be times when you face a devil, a demon, a dark cosmic force, that just won't surrender victory to you. What do you do then?**

Some people spend their whole lives fighting the same spiritual battles. That's a shame. While you are fighting the same old battles, you become ineffective at achieving a newer, higher level of spiritual warfare where you could be a better witness, have a stronger testimony, experience a greater anointing, worship at a higher level and see greater battles won for the kingdom of God. To put it bluntly; **lives are being destroyed by sin and souls are going to hell all around you while you are still struggling with the same old devils and battles over and over and over.**

What kind of battles? Habitual sin; filthy addictions to cigarettes, drugs, or alcohol; depression, unforgiveness, hurt feelings, bitterness...I think you know what I'm talking about. Everything else may be fine in your life, but this one battle has continued on for years.

The Apostles of our Lord experienced such an experience in Matthew chapter 17. They had tried to cast a devil out of a boy that his father had brought to them. Then Jesus said, *"bring him hither to me"* and He cast the devil out of the lunatic son.

Then the disciples asked, *"Why could we not cast him out?"* Jesus said, *"because of your unbelief."* And then he added, *"Howbeit, this kind goeth not out but my prayer and fasting."* (Matthew 17:18-21).

We know that the disciples were not accustomed to much prayer and fasting because in Matthew chapter 9, the disciples of John asked Jesus why His disciples didn't fast like the Pharisees and the disciples of John. Jesus responded that as long as the bridegroom was with them they wouldn't fast, but that they would after He was taken away.

So, we see that fasting was not one of their disciplines yet. And while they had been given power in Matthew chapter 10 to heal the sick, cleanse the lepers, raise the dead, cast out devils... they now face a devil that requires a deeper walk, a higher anointing, and a richer experience with godliness, if you please. **They were going to have to add fasting to their prayer life if they were going to reach that level of devils.**

Are you up against a wall in your walk with God? Perhaps for years you have languished in spiritual laziness because you couldn't get past the present level of spiritual attack. Well, it's time for a change. I'm preaching something that has changed my life and I believe it will change yours.

"This kind goeth not out but by prayer and fasting." What kind? **The kind you can't overcome at the level you're at.** Dedicate yourself, right now, to more prayer, and more skipped meals. Prayer and fasting will change your life and set you free by those weapons that are mighty through God to the pulling down of strongholds.

Prayer and Fasting—Part 3

We sing about victory in Jesus. We sing about the power that's in the shed blood of Jesus Christ. We preach about spiritual authority and demon-chasing power. We have learned about deliverance through the Word of God. Life changing Scriptures such as Mark 9:23, *"Jesus said unto him, If thou canst believe, all things are possible to him that believeth."* Or, Hebrews 11:1, *"Now faith is the substance of things hoped for, the evidence of things not seen."* We rejoice with great joy when God comes through, often just in time. And we rejoice again when God makes a way where there seemed to be no way.

There are Bible stories after Bible stories of great triumphs over evil as God's children fought against incredible odds and God wrought great victories. How can you not rejoice with the three Hebrew children who came through the fiery furnace untouched by the fire, or Daniel who survived the night in the lion's den, or the stories of the anointed prophets and the incredible miracles that they performed by their faith in a God who cannot fail! What about the mighty works of the Apostles who, the Bible said, *"went forth, and preached everywhere, the Lord working with them, and confirming the word with signs following. Amen"* (See Mark 16:20). We read in Acts 5:12-16, *"And by the hands of the apostles were many signs and wonders wrought among the people; (and they were all with one accord in Solomon's porch. And of the rest durst no man join himself*

91

to them: but the people magnified them. And believers were the more added to the Lord, multitudes both of men and women.) Insomuch that they brought forth the sick into the streets, and laid them on beds and couches, that at the least the shadow of Peter passing by might overshadow some of them. There came also a multitude out of the cities round about unto Jerusalem, bringing sick folks, and them which were vexed with unclean spirits: and they were healed every one." And Jesus told of the empowerment of believers in Acts 16:17-18, *"And these signs shall follow them that believe; In my name shall they cast out devils; they shall speak with new tongues; They shall take up serpents; and if they drink any deadly thing, it shall not hurt them; they shall lay hands on the sick, and they shall recover."*

This kind of apostolic power is still available and intended for the church today! But, every time we read of a miracle in the Bible, we are witnessing an impossible situation. Every time God came through with a miraculous answer, there was an impossible situation that drove men and women to their knees in prayer and fasting. **Miracles do not often come without someone earnestly seeking God and believing that their seeking is worth the time**. Someone once said that the reason people don't pray is because they don't think it's worth their time.

I believe that God will take care of His children. But, I also believe that suffering, persecution, pain, and heartache are part of the cross that God's children sometimes have to carry. Those who are required to carry such crosses are molded into powerful vessels of spiritual power that God can use.

The big problem is that because of a lack of commitment, **too many people walk away from their faith when the going gets tough**. Too many people are not conditioned to understand that sometimes you have to climb the mountain like Abraham did with Isaac. Sometimes you have to go into the fiery furnace. Sometimes you will be tossed into the lion's den. **But, thank God, that's when you see the miracles!** That's when God comes through. And, God gets all the glory! God is absolutely the deliverer! Man will not and cannot receive any glory through situations like that.

There will be times when the walls won't come tumbling down immediately. There will be times when the healing won't come instantly and when deliverance is a slow process. **There will be situations where faith is tested and commitment becomes vital to victory.**

I've used the example of the disciples trying to cast out a demon and being unsuccessful. Jesus said it was because that kind of problem required prayer and fasting. So, yes, that demon can be cast out. But, they would have to change their approach. **How often do we keep doing the same thing and expect different results?**

Pray a little harder. Fast a little more. Worship until you give Him high praise! Praises higher than you've ever given God before! It may involve finances, time, effort, helping the poor, or sending missionaries around the globe. Do something different. Do something bigger.

Jesus said, "This kind!" What kind? The kind you can't get victory over. The walls you can't bring down. The feelings you can't conquer. The pain you can't heal. The bitterness you can't forget. The unforgiveness that just won't let go.

I'm challenging someone to keep up the attack. Stay the course. **There is victory in Jesus!** There is power in the blood. There is peace for the troubled mind. There is healing for the broken body. **There is a miracle with your name on it!**

Yes, it may require a season of searching; a season of prayer and fasting; a season of seeking God with all of your heart, soul, mind and strength. Am I saying this to discourage you? No, you're already discouraged. I'm saying it to encourage you! Don't give up. Don't give in. Don't let go of your faith. Get back up, get back to church, get back in the Word, lift up your hands and praise Him! God is an awesome God!

Prayer Cloths

Christians have long noted the healing effect that prayer cloths have when prayed over and anointed with oil. When a person cannot be in the presence of those wishing to pray for him, an anointed cloth may be sent to that person. God has honored that faith time and time again.

One example of a miracle, as the result of a prayer cloth being used, was when a dog recently mauled a local 4-year-old girl and a large chunk of her face was disfigured. The doctors said that nerves were destroyed and she would never be able to have feeling in her right cheek, nor would she have a smile. But, on the night of her attack, one of our ministry assistants and his wife joined me in driving to Nashville to pray for a miracle for this child. We anointed a prayer cloth and left it with her while she lay in Vanderbilt hospital.

The little girl took the prayer cloth and put it in the hands of a teddy bear on her own pillow. She would pick up the prayer cloth, rub it on her hurting face, and say that Jesus was going to heal her. Then she would lay the cloth back in the paws of that teddy bear.

Guess what? God did an incredible miracle on her face, and yes, she has a smile!

Do you think that was an accident? Was that just a natural occurrence? None of the family, nor our church family, nor this preacher believes that it was just a lucky break for the doctors. No, I don't think so. I know, beyond the shadow of a doubt, that through the stripes that Jesus Christ bore at His trial and crucifixion, God healed her! All through obedience to the Word of God and faith in something we read in His Word.

Acts 19:11-12, *"And God wrought special miracles by the hands of Paul: So that from his body were brought unto the sick handkerchiefs or aprons, and the diseases departed from them, and the evil spirits went out of them."*

The anointing of God was somehow resident in those handkerchiefs or aprons and caused diseases to depart from the diseased, and evil spirits were caused to depart from those who were possessed by the devil. We know that the woman with the issue of blood came from behind Him, Jesus Christ, and touched the hem of His garment and was made whole.

We also know that we have the right to expect healing for our physical bodies. *"Who hath believed our report? and to whom is the arm of the LORD revealed? For he shall grow up before him as a tender plant, and as a root out of a dry ground: he hath no form nor comeliness; and when we shall see him, there is no beauty that we should desire him. He is despised and rejected of men; a man of sorrows, and acquainted with grief: and we hid as it were our faces from him; he was despised, and we esteemed him not. Surely he hath borne our griefs, and carried our sorrows: yet we did esteem him stricken, smitten of God, and afflicted. But he was wounded for our transgressions, he was bruised for our iniquities: the chastisement of our peace was upon him; and with his stripes we are healed"* (Isaiah 53:1-5).

And, again in 1Peter 2:24, *"Who his own self bare our sins in his own body on the tree, that we, being dead to sins, should live unto righteousness: by whose stripes ye were healed."*

Much of Christ's ministry was spent healing the sick. When Jesus passed by the cripples walked. When Jesus passed by the blind saw. When Jesus passed by the sick were healed and He still is doing the same today. There is nothing in the Scripture that suggests that miracles were to stop after the Apostles died. The truth is that the Word is adamant about believers having such power! Mark 16:17-18, *"And these signs shall follow them that believe; In my name shall they cast out devils; they shall speak with new tongues; They shall take up serpents; and if they drink any deadly thing, it shall not hurt them; they shall lay hands on the sick, and they shall recover."*

Prayer cloths are a wonderful way to take healing for the body, soul and spirit to people that are hurting. Our church has distributed hundreds of prayer cloths over the last several years to people needing a touch from the Lord with wonderful testimonies of God's healing and deliverance. Likewise, hundreds of prayer cloths have been given to people at our thrift store, Sacks Thrift Avenue, while ministering to people there. Only eternity will tell the impact that the prayer of faith and anointing of oil on a prayer cloth has had on people's lives.

Our Reaction to God's Love

He saved me. That is God's love in action! *"But God commendeth his love toward us, in that, while we were yet sinners, Christ died for us"* (Romans 5:8).

The story of the Bible is God's unconditional love. God is love. No other religion in the world has a God of love. God is a Spirit, and yet He loved us so much that He came to us, robed Himself in human flesh to offer Himself as a sacrifice for the sins of mankind. *"For God so loved the world, that he gave his only begotten Son, that whosoever believeth in him should not perish, but have everlasting life" (*John 3:16).

So, what is to be our response to such love? How do we react to such a God? Again, the Bible is plain and direct as to how we should respond. Perhaps the summary of that response is stated in this command. *"And one of the scribes came, and having heard them reasoning together, and perceiving that he had answered them well, asked him, Which is the first commandment of all? And Jesus answered him, The first of all the commandments is, Hear, O Israel; The Lord our God is one Lord: And thou shalt love the Lord thy God with all thy heart, and with all thy soul, and with all thy mind, and with all thy strength: this is the first commandment" (Mark 12:28-30).*

This Scripture should remove all questions as to what our response should be to God's amazing love and grace to us. **To assume that**

99

all we have to do is to believe that He died for us is absurd in the light of this verse. To assume that we can live the way we want to and still have a mansion just over the hilltop is presumptuous. To live our life for ourselves and then at the end of our life, when the candle of our life is blown out, to blow the smoke in God's face and say, "I'm coming home" is beyond comprehension to those who know and understand the Scriptures.

Making Heaven our home is the result of accepting the death, burial, and resurrection of our Lord and Savior by being born again of the water and the Spirit (See Acts 2:38) and then living for Him in holiness, in purity, and in godliness for the rest of our lives. **We are to love God in return for His goodness to us with all of our heart, soul, mind and strength**. That covers just about all of our life doesn't it?

My very being, my thoughts, my strength, or in other words, my actions are what God requires. He said it Himself. **This is the first commandment, the most important commandment of life.**

Yes, He saved me! Now, I will live for Him!

Nothing

Bro. Ron Macy of Houston, Texas preached a wonderful sermon at a camp meeting service in Nashville. His message title was "Nothing" which inspired me and I hope will bless you. His text was in I Kings 18:42-43, *"So Ahab went up to eat and to drink. And Elijah went up to the top of Carmel; and he cast himself down upon the earth, and put his face between his knees, And said to his servant, Go up now, look toward the sea. And he went up, and looked, and said, There is nothing. And he said, Go again seven times."*

How is your faith? What about your faith? Do you have questions, fears, discouragement or depression?

Think for a moment about the prophet Elijah. He had prophesied to the king that it was going to rain. They had just endured a 3 1/2 year drought. But, now it was going to rain. The prophets of Baal had been defeated. God had shown up and sent fire from heaven and vindicated the faith of Elijah. Now the man of God was praying for rain—rain that God had promised.

But, he still had to pray. God has given us many promises, and you may have received a word from God assuring you that your miracle was on its way. But, you still have to seek God's face. **There are many enemies of your soul and often you've got to enter into the spiritual warfare, spiritual battles of prayer, fasting and faith to see your miracles come to birth.**

Elijah prayed and then sent his servant to look toward the sea. He was looking for signs of rain. Some clouds if you please. But, the servant came back and said, *"Nothing. There is nothing."*

How do you handle that kind of disappointment? Nothing. Nothing's happening. No sign of an answer. No sign of a healing. No sign of a financial breakthrough. No sign of a healed relationship; nothing. We've all lived through times when nothing was happening! How do you handle that? Do you get mad at God? Do you get upset at the preacher? Do you get bitter at the church? **When there is nothing, what do you do?**

Well, Elijah knew what to do. **He said, "Go again!"** Elijah didn't give up. He knew what God had said. So, he said, "Go again." We have the Word of God today. **We know what the Bible says. So, go again.**

How many times do you GO AGAIN? Elijah sent his servant until the answer came! I don't believe there is a time limit. We're only limited by our faith. Go again! No sign of an answer yet? Go again! Look again! Pray again. Go to church again. Fast again. Give your tithe and offerings again! Worship again. Cry aloud again.

The servant came back again and said there is nothing. Elijah said, "Go again!" The servant said there is nothing. Elijah said, "Go again!" The servant said there is nothing!

I think you're getting the picture by now. The key to receiving our miracle from God is to keep asking. Look again! It doesn't really matter how many times you have to ask or go look for an answer. You just keep looking. God will always come through.

Perhaps it's a prayer about an unsaved loved one. Nothing? Go again! Maybe it's a prayer about your backslidden children. Nothing? Go again! Are you seeking God for guidance and direction? Nothing? Go again! Do you seek for peace of mind? Nothing? Go again! Ask again. Has disease invaded your body and you really believe in divine healing, but there is no sign of an answer? Nothing. Go back to the altar again. Call for the elders again. Be anointed with oil again.

Just what do you do when there is no answer to your prayer? The answer is to go again! You just never quit. You don't give up.

Even though Joshua had a word of direction from God, it still took a lot of faith to march around Jericho six days...and nothing! And, then, more faith to walk around that city six times on the seventh day. Nothing! Nothing at all. No sign of victory. No sign of God's Word being fulfilled. But, hang on! Guess what happened on the seventh time! The walls came tumbling down and a great victory was wrought.

It's true that great victories are seldom won quickly. It's the made up mind that insures the faith to go again!

So, it doesn't matter how many days or weeks or months or years... that there is nothing. Go again! The answer is on the way!

Spiritual Warfare and Unity

When God speaks to the church we should always remember and appreciate what God has said or done through His Word or His Gifts. I want to share with you a couple of the messages that God has sent to our church.

One of the first things God made me to realize was that we were involved in serious spiritual warfare.

In Ephesians 6:12, *"For we wrestle not against flesh and blood, but against principalities, against powers, against the rulers of the darkness of this world, against spiritual wickedness in high places."*

This verse means that there are demons, evil spirits and Satan himself who is attacking the church.

When I came to pastor the First UPC of Greenfield, I made up my mind that I would find out why so many said that there couldn't be a Pentecostal revival in Greenfield.

Well, it didn't take long until I began to realize that Satan was on the attack with strong spiritual warfare.

It was at this point that someone put me on to the fact that we live in a part of the country known, by a governor's decree in 1952, as the Kingdom of Skullbonia. From roughly the Tennessee River, west to the Mississippi River in Northwest Tennessee, it is officially known as the Kingdom of Skullbonia. Look it up on the Internet. You can Google Kingdom of Skullbonia and get a lot of information including a glimpse into the sins of the past: the sins of the land that has created a brass ceiling, as it were, keeping the gospel seed from flourishing in people's lives as it should, because the rain of the Holy Ghost has been hindered through the Prince of the Kingdom of Skullbonia.

It's not always that we are given the name of spirits to attack through prayer. But thank God, this prince is coming down, or more correctly, is being hindered; is being relocated; is being crippled by the prayers of praying people in Northwest Tennessee and the rain of the Holy Ghost is falling.

The spiritual brass ceiling is opening and we are witnessing break-throughs in the Kingdom of God with a greater spiritual hunger among God's people. More souls are being added to the Kingdom of God as He is building His church and the gates of hell are not going to prevail against it. Or, to put it another way, as the church moves forward toward hell's authority, hell will not be able to stop us!

Spiritual warfare affects individuals, families, churches, preachers; literally anyone who is trying to please God! You need to realize that the devil is fighting you and you must resist him.

So, firstly, here in Greenfield, I realized that we were involved in serious spiritual warfare that required drastic measures of prayer, fasting, a strong measure of faith, and a complete trust in the Word of God.

Secondly, the Lord has wonderfully and powerfully revealed to me and our church body the necessity and power of unity.

In Psalms 133:1-3 we read, *"Behold, how good and how pleasant it is for brethren to dwell together in unity! It is like the precious ointment upon the head, that ran down upon the beard, even Aaron's beard: that went down to the skirts of his garments; As the dew of Hermon, and as the dew that descended upon the mountains of Zion: for there the LORD commanded the blessing, even life for evermore."*

You can have all truth. You can have great organization. You can have outstanding music. You can have anointed preaching. **But, without unity the blessing of God cannot flow, the anointing cannot bless and God is hindered from working in your behalf.**

Notice the Scripture, *"for there the Lord commanded the blessing."* Where does the Lord command the blessing? Where unity is! Where there is unity, God can work.

Having unity doesn't mean that we all think alike. **It means we have the love of God and we care for each other and have a right spirit, preferring one another.**

Unity in a church needs to be protected. Unity in a body of believers needs to be valued. Every member needs to work to insure unity in every situation. Problems can be solved without destroying a church's unity. This also is not just about church unity. The same holds true in a marriage, a family, a relationship. *"Can two walk together, except they be agreed?"* (Amos 3:3).

I believe that one of the greatest problems in churches today is the lack of unity. A Biblical unity would create an atmosphere where apostolic doctrine could be preached and practiced. Biblical unity would create a spiritual power that would enable God to pour out of His Spirit upon us in a measure that would break the strongholds of Satan and set the captive free!

Yes, there is indeed a war taking place for the souls of men and women.

One of the greatest tools in spiritual warfare is unity among any entity. There God commands the blessing!

Three Key Spiritual Weapons

I am always thrilled when I read in Acts 5: 12-16, *"And by the hands of the apostles were many signs and wonders wrought among the people; (and they were all with one accord in Solomon's porch. And of the rest durst no man join himself to them: but the people magnified them. And believers were the more added to the Lord, multitudes both of men and women.) Insomuch that they brought forth the sick into the streets, and laid them on beds and couches, that at the least the shadow of Peter passing by might overshadow some of them. There came also a multitude out of the cities round about unto Jerusalem, bringing sick folks, and them which were vexed with unclean spirits: and they were healed every one."*

We know that these experiences were just not consigned to the first church.

Mark 16:15-20, *"And he said unto them, Go ye into all the world, and preach the gospel to every creature. He that believeth and is baptized shall be saved; but he that believeth not shall be damned. And these signs shall follow them that believe; In my name shall they cast out devils; they shall speak with new tongues; They shall take up serpents; and if they drink any deadly thing, it shall not hurt them; they shall lay hands on the sick, and they shall recover.*

So then after the Lord had spoken unto them, he was received up into heaven, and sat on the right hand of God. And they went forth, and preached everywhere, the Lord working with them, and confirming the word with signs following. Amen."

The church today has the same opportunity for spiritual power as the first church did in the book of Acts. Some may not possess it, but we have the same opportunity. How do I know this today? Because the Bible says so!

More than anything else in this world, I want to see a demonstration of His power in these last days to empower the church to bring in the harvest. The fields are ready to be harvested. We are to pray for laborers to work in the harvest. Many people won't get involved in the harvest because they don't have the saving and enabling power of the Holy Ghost in their own lives.

There are three notable spiritual weapons that the early church had that still belong to the Church today. The signs, wonders and miracles that were wrought by the early Apostles, disciples, and followers of Christ were made possible by at least these three weapons: the Word, the Name, and the Holy Ghost.

First of all, they had the Word: the Word of God, the message of salvation through Jesus Christ. No, they didn't have the Bible as we have it; they were actually living out the writing of the New Testament. But, they had the message of the good news of the death, burial and resurrection of Jesus Christ.

"Then Philip went down to the city of Samaria, and preached Christ unto them. And the people with one accord gave heed unto those things which Philip spake, hearing and seeing the miracles which he did. For unclean spirits, crying with loud voice, came out of many that were possessed with them: and many taken with palsies, and that were lame, were healed. And there was great joy in that city" (Acts 8:5-8).

The preaching of the Word of God brought these miracles and conversions! Many other instances in the book of Acts bear out the importance of the Word of God in bringing a manifestation of His power into His church and His work.

The second thing was the Name! The only saving name in the universe: Jesus!

"Then Peter said, Silver and gold have I none; but such as I have give I thee: In the name of Jesus Christ of Nazareth rise up and walk" (Acts 3:6)

Throughout the early days of the church, it was the name that brought the power.

Acts 4:12 tells us why. *"Neither is there salvation in any other: for there is none other name under heaven given among men, whereby we must be saved."*

The third powerful weapon against Satan was the Holy Spirit, the Spirit of God. *"And when they had prayed, the place was shaken where they were assembled together; and they were all filled with the Holy Ghost, and they spake the word of God with boldness"* (Acts 4:31).

Men filled with the Holy Ghost discerned and cast out devils, healed the sick, raised the dead and prayed until the heavens were shaken. Paul and Silas sang and prayed until the prison doors were opened!

Church, we have the same power today. **The Word, the Name, and the Spirit!**

Deception—Part One

A friend called me this week and asked me if I had heard about some mutual acquaintances which had departed from the faith to join a movement that denies the new birth experience and disregards personal holiness and separation from the world, among other doctrinal abominations. Yes, I had heard. He asked me, "What is going on?" He asked, "How could this be? What are they thinking?" Our conversation ended on a note of caution, of realizing that if these could be deceived, then who among us couldn't be?

The Bible says in Matthew 24:24, *"For there shall arise false Christs, and false prophets, and shall shew great signs and wonders; insomuch that, if it were possible, they shall deceive the very elect."*

The implication is that even those who are very well grounded in the Scriptures must be careful; because through signs and wonders shown by false christs and false prophets, many will be deceived. **If a person's life is not consistent with the written Word of God, it doesn't matter what kind of signs and wonders they can do; they're wrong and they can lead you astray.**

I believe in signs and wonders. I believe in the miraculous. But, folks, your soul's salvation is not based upon following signs and wonders. **Signs and wonders are to follow you!** Your faith must be based upon the precious Word of God! The Word of God is the only thing that will keep you from being deceived.

When people start telling you that you can skip a certain part of the Bible, or that a certain part doesn't pertain to today's church, you're in trouble. **We need the full gospel**. And the full gospel is the only gospel! The full gospel is what was experienced by the first church as recorded in the Book of Acts.

I'm afraid that using excuses of tradition and inconvenience won't cut it at the judgment bar. Telling God that you just didn't see it His way is going to sound pretty feeble on that great and final day.

A woman told me that she knew she needed to go to church (she doesn't go at all). But, with that said, she informed me that the devil didn't have her. I'm thinking that she is grossly deceived. I told her she needed to be in the house of God. I see her at the post office. I see her at the grocery. But, I don't see her at church. How can she explain that to God? It appears to me that she knows that if she went to church she would become accountable to others. She would have to change her lifestyle and evidently she isn't willing to do that.

"Be not deceived; God is not mocked: for whatsoever a man soweth, that shall he also reap" (Galatians 6:7).

"Know ye not that the unrighteous shall not inherit the kingdom of God? Be not deceived: neither fornicators, nor idolaters, nor adulterers, nor effeminate, nor abusers of themselves with mankind, Nor thieves, nor covetous, nor drunkards, nor revilers, nor extortioners, shall inherit the kingdom of God. And such were some of you: but ye are washed, but ye are sanctified, but ye are justified in the name of the Lord Jesus, and by the Spirit of our God" (I Corinthians 6:9-11).

Notice, such *were* some of you. You're not now! **After you are washed, sanctified and justified, you quit doing those things!** You can't make it to heaven if you keep doing those things!

There are over 60 other verses about deception and the possibility that in the last days you might fall to deception and be lost for eternity. **Deception is the inability to discern between right and wrong.** For many people today, there is no wrong, there is no sin, there is no evil. That's being deceived. Somehow you think you'll sneak into heaven on perhaps your mother's faith, or somehow God understands your situation. Yes, He understands your situation. That's why He said, *"Repent, and be baptized every one of you in the name of Jesus Christ for the remission of sins, and ye shall receive the gift of the Holy Ghost"* (Acts 2:38).

Don't be deceived!

Deception—Part 2

To keep from being deceived, we must be able to discern between right and wrong. We must be aware of things that are holy and things that are profane. We must discern the righteous and the unrighteous.

Hebrews 5:14 tells us that *"Strong meat belongeth to them that are of full age, even those who by reason of use have their senses exercised to discern both good and evil."*

Over and over we are admonished to not be deceived in the last days. Most Christians recognize that the often prophesied last days are upon us. The Apocalypse described in the book of Revelation is unfolding before our very eyes.

In Matthew chapter 4 we read, *4 "And Jesus answered and said unto them, Take heed that no man deceive you. 5 For many shall come in my name, saying, I am Christ; and shall deceive many."*

11 "And many false prophets shall rise, and shall deceive many."

24 "For there shall arise false christs, and false prophets, and shall shew great signs and wonders; insomuch that, if it were possible, they shall deceive the very elect."

How can a Christian be deceived into believing a lie? How can a Christian be deceived into following a false minister?

In II Thessalonians chapter 2 we read where those who received not the love of the truth will be sent a strong delusion, that they should believe a lie, because they had pleasure in unrighteousness.

There are many ways in which a person can be deceived, but one of the most obvious is not caring about, or not discerning between good and evil. I think this reflects the age in which we live. When you read through the prophets in the Old Testament they often lamented how that Israel called the bad good. The prophets complained that the people as a whole stopped discerning between the holy and the profane. This is what we are facing today! There are so few preachers, let alone saints, who will stand up and call sin, sin! There are so few who dare to buck the socially correct crowd and stand for Bible holiness, Bible morality, Bible standards, and clear Bible doctrine!

We must be able to discern between good and evil. One ministry leader even went so far as to say that when the antichrist comes, many Christians will be taken in because of lack of discernment.

Let's quit thinking about offending someone, and let's be truthful. For example, a homosexual is committing an abomination unto God. But, because of political correctness, society has given the stamp of approval for this obvious perversion. We need to put down all the crazy arguments about rights and societal advances. When things are wrong, they are wrong. Nature teaches us that we are fools to think otherwise.

It gets right down to where we live in Northwest Tennessee. It's wrong to go out in public half naked. It's wrong to lie, cheat, steal, fornicate, and commit adultery. So it's wrong to live together without being married. Everyone knows it, but, no one will say it. Few will preach it!

So, why are there so many Christians being deceived by apparent sin and calling wrong right? I'll give you one reason. **Too many confessing Christians have never been born again.** They've confessed Christ, but never went on to be born again of the water and the Spirit. In other words, there has been limited conversion: just enough for some preacher to assure them they're saved, but not enough for their life to change. Not enough to be converted into disciples of Jesus Christ.

Many denominational leaders readily admit that a vast majority of their church's membership have never been born again. Surveys show that 97% of those who have "accepted Christ" do not have a different world view than non-professing people which is why people can't discern between good and evil today. Their heart is still evil. The old man still rules. And, that means they are not saved from the judgment of sin to come. That means eternity in hell, not heaven.

Are you born again? Have you received the Holy Ghost since you believed?

Deception—Part 3

There are certain laws and principles of God that will never be broken or changed. God's moral laws are settled. For instance, God's love is unchangeable. Likewise, God's judgments are sure and righteous. Saint or sinner, these laws are immutable. They will not change.

One such law is stated in Galatians 6:7, *"Be not deceived; God is not mocked: for whatsoever a man soweth, that shall he also reap."*

Take note of the Beatitudes from Matthew chapter 5,

3 "Blessed are the poor in spirit: for theirs is the kingdom of heaven.

4 Blessed are they that mourn: for they shall be comforted.

5 Blessed are the meek: for they shall inherit the earth.

6 Blessed are they which do hunger and thirst after righteousness: for they shall be filled.

7 Blessed are the merciful: for they shall obtain mercy.

8 Blessed are the pure in heart: for they shall see God.

9 Blessed are the peacemakers: for they shall be called the children of God."

All of this is about reaping what you've sown—the truth the Bible teaches about sowing and reaping.

According to the Word of God, this generation, the one that will see the Second Coming of the Lord, is very susceptible to being deceived. I don't want to be deceived and miss what God has for me in this life or, worse yet, miss Heaven by being deceived.

Look what Hosea says in Hosea 8:7, *"For they have sown the wind, and they shall reap the whirlwind: it hath no stalk: the bud shall yield no meal: if so be it yield, the strangers shall swallow it up."*

The phrase *sown the wind* is a proverbial way of saying that the effort is a lost labor. **It is referring to a person making senseless prayers for a good harvest when he has sown bad seed.** And, on the spiritual application, one commentator writes that sowing the wind is to make a vain show of worship, while faith and obedience are wanting. Always remember this: **Worship requires a sacrifice.** I'm not just talking about getting out of bed on Sunday morning and dragging yourself to the house of God. The Bible says that we are to, *"offer our bodies as a living sacrifice, holy and acceptable unto God, which is our reasonable service"* (Romans 12:1).

Sowing the wind can be done in so many different ways, but basically it means that we are planting seeds that are not going to bring forth a good or pleasant harvest. It's time wasted. It's effort ruined. It is a sacrifice that God will not accept. Wow, that's a whole subject in itself isn't it: **a sacrifice that God will not accept.** God demands our sacrifice to Him be complete, whole, holy, unblemished, from a pure heart, not just from the lips. God will not accept a sick calf or a crippled lamb! I realize that this is a subject that not too many are familiar with today, but it's still the truth!

Here is some more truth. Your salvation is not just dependent upon you accepting Jesus Christ, it's also about Him accepting You!!

II Corinthians 6:17-18, *"Wherefore come out from among them, and be ye separate, saith the Lord, and touch not the unclean thing; and I will receive you, And will be a Father unto you, and ye shall be my sons and daughters, saith the Lord Almighty."*

A relationship with God demands separation from the world!

Hosea 8:7, *"For they have sown the wind, and they shall reap the whirlwind..."* The Bible is saying that there are those who will live their life to please themselves and that they will reap destruction.

God loves you. In that truth there is no doubt. But, please know, that doesn't save you. The blood must be applied. The Israelites not only killed the sacrificial Lamb on that first Passover, they also applied the blood to their doorposts. It wouldn't have mattered that the blood was even in their house, it had to be applied. You may know all about God, and the sacrifice that He gave for your life, but, that doesn't save you. **The blood must be applied through obedience and faith.**

Yes, God loves you. But, if you sow the wind, you will reap a whirlwind. Don't doubt it. Don't blame someone else for the bad things that are happening to you. You are just reaping what you have sown. Do not be deceived, God is not mocked. You WILL reap what you have sown.

A person can't spend their teenage years in mockery of God's laws, and then expect to enjoy a good life. A life filled with drugs, alcohol, and immorality will not produce a harvest conducive to Godly principles. A young girl cannot give her life to a drug addict or an alcoholic and not expect abuse, poverty, and disease! Need I go on? Sow the wind, and reap the whirlwind. Do not doubt God's Word. You will not be an exception! Can God forgive? Of course. But, many, many people who come to know the Lord, having being born again of the water and the Spirit (see Acts 2:38), still live out the rest of their lives reaping from the bad seed that they have sown. Will God help? Yes, His grace will bring a person through, but, oh my, the pain and heartache that must be borne. My heart aches at times for young people that I see making such bad decisions and choices in their young lives.

Do not be deceived. If you sow to the wind you will reap the whirlwind!

Deception—Part 4

One of the most repeated warnings in the Bible about living in the last days is to not be deceived. Matthew 24, Luke 21, II Corinthians 11 and other references point out a very real danger that will come to believers in the last days. Deception—a scary word. In context of the Scriptures, deception would mean that a person would leave the pure doctrine of truth and pursue the teachings of men. And, of course, the end result of that would mean that a person's soul would be lost by following error instead of God's truth. Let's read some Scripture.

II Thessalonians 2: 9-12, *"Even him, whose coming is after the working of Satan with all power and signs and lying wonders, And with all deceivableness of unrighteousness in them that perish; because they received not the love of the truth, that they might be saved. And for this cause God shall send them strong delusion, that they should believe a lie: That they all might be damned who believed not the truth, but had pleasure in unrighteousness."*

John 14:6, *"Jesus saith unto him, I am the way, the truth, and the life: no man cometh unto the Father, but by me."*

The truth is declared in the Bible, God's Holy Word. Our responsibility is to rightly divide the Word, or to understand what is written that we might have eternal life through Jesus Christ.

Four times the phrase "sound doctrine" is mentioned in the Bible. One meaning of the Greek word used for "sound" is "to be uncorrupt" (Strong's). What we believe must be pure and whole.

Does it matter what a person believes? Well, the Bible says it does! **Contrary to current Christian culture, what you believe determines how you live, how you worship, where you go to church, and what you believe determines where you will spend eternity.** Please, don't let anyone tell you that it doesn't matter what you believe. Folks, according to God's truth, you can be sincerely wrong!

Then how could a person be deceived? Wouldn't there be a warning; a bad feeling? Evangelist Lee Stoneking says this: **"Revelation and deception have the same feeling."**

In other words, do not be deceived by new ideas, new thoughts, new doctrines, or new beliefs that are contrary to the revealed Word of God! It may have a good feeling and appeal to your flesh, but if it's against the Word of God, run from it! Do not be deceived! Remember, revelation and deception have the same feeling.

Don't allow feelings to guide your belief system. You can't trust your feelings because they change daily. But, you can trust the Word of God! It never changes! Just because something feels right doesn't mean it is right!

If someone tells you that the Church is outdated and not needed anymore, do not be deceived. The Bible still says in Hebrew 10:25, *"Not forsaking the assembling of ourselves together, as the manner of some is; but exhorting one another: and so much the more, as ye see the day approaching."* As the day of the Lord approaches, there will be a deceiving spirit telling people that they don't need to assemble together in worship. Don't believe it! Do not be deceived. You need the church!

If someone tells you there's more than one road to Heaven do not be deceived! Acts 4:12 says, *"Neither is there salvation in any other: for there is none other name under heaven given among men, whereby we must be saved."* Run from deception! Run to the Word! The Truth is what will save you!

If someone tells you that the Bible way of salvation is outdated and old fashioned, do not be deceived. The Bible still says in Acts 2:38, *"Then Peter said unto them, Repent, and be baptized every one of you in the name of Jesus Christ for the remission of sins, and ye shall receive the gift of the Holy Ghost."*

Galatians 1:8, *"But though we, or an angel from heaven, preach any other gospel unto you than that which we have preached unto you, let him be accursed."*

What you believe must be what the Apostles and early disciples of the book of Acts believed. **Your born again, salvation experience should be the same as what the converts in the early church believed.** If someone comes preaching anything less, do not be deceived!

Matthew 24:4-5, *"And Jesus answered and said unto them, Take heed that no man deceive you. For many shall come in my name, saying, I am Christ; and shall deceive many."* Many will come preaching false doctrines and claiming to be of Christ. Do not be deceived!

Matthew 7:21-23, *"Not everyone that saith unto me, Lord, Lord, shall enter into the kingdom of heaven; but he that doeth the will of my Father which is in heaven. Many will say to me in that day, Lord, Lord, have we not prophesied in thy name? and in thy name have cast out devils? and in thy name done many wonderful works? And then will I profess unto them, I never knew you: depart from me, ye that work iniquity."*

The criteria for God's judgment will be "ye that work iniquity." If a person is still living in sin, they are not saved.

Denying the Power Thereof

At a recent revival service in central Illinois, a United Methodist evangelist from Australia told of how God spoke to him on 9/11 while watching the TV coverage of the terrorist attacks in America and told him to come to America as a missionary. While preaching this past week, he told of how people have asked him, "What are the differences you see between the church in Australia and the church in America?" His comment was, "In Australia you can tell a person is a Christian by looking at them. In America, there is no difference between the appearance of a Christian and the rest of the world."

His remarks are an indictment to Bible believing people. **God's people have always been and, in reality, will always be a separated people.** God intends for there to be a difference between the clean and the unclean: a difference between the holy and unholy and righteousness and unrighteousness. To call on the name of God without being separated from the world is hypocrisy.

I've noticed a cry coming from denominational and charismatic leaders for the church to return to holiness. As an example, Lee Grady, editor of Charisma magazine, sent out an online editorial titled, "The Fire of Holiness vs. the Spirit of Perversion." In this article he bemoans the fact of another well-known preacher being accused of perversion. He cries out that "moral failure in our ranks has become an epidemic—and the only solution is a heaven-sent spiritual housecleaning". He continues: "We must preach the full gospel,

129

not a neutered version that avoids any mention of sin, judgment or holiness. The redemption of Jesus does not give us a license to sin, and those who teach such heresy will be held especially liable."

There have been many godly preachers, men of God, who have been crying out against the perversion of the American church for years, as standards of conduct, standards of morality, and standards of dress have been not only dropped, but ridiculed...BY THE CHURCH! Thank God for those who have still been preaching this truth of separation from worldliness by the Church.

But, the mainstream church in America is in big trouble.

What has happened? How could things like this, and much worse, be happening in professing Christian's lives?

Liberal Christians, for many years now, have degraded anyone who would preach holiness standards as being legalistic. So, the nation's pulpits have largely grown silent on the subject. And, look where it's taken us. Look at your choir this morning in your church. Does the appearance and dress speak of holiness to you? I hope so. Do the saints of God, those professing to be living their lives for God... does their appearance mirror a relationship with God through purity, holiness, godliness? Must we continue with our head in the sand, or can there be a revival of holiness? And, please don't give me this stuff of "God doesn't care what you look like on the outside—it's the inside that counts." Where did that ever come from? Common sense shows that a person can readily tell what's on the inside by what's on the outside. Faith without corresponding works is deception (See James 2:20).

Let's go to II Timothy 3:5, *"Having a form of godliness, but denying the power thereof: from such turn away."* **The power of the gospel is the result of being converted from a sinner to a child of God.** To deny that power is to say, I will do things my way, not God's way. To deny that power is to reject the Word of the Lord, and still profess godliness.

One of the most obvious, but seldom stated problems in the American church today is this. **Too many people profess Christianity but have never been born again.** Too many believers have never been converted! They've been told that believing is all there is to the Gospel.

Acts 2:38 still says, *"Repent, and be baptized every one of you in the name of Jesus Christ for the remission of sins, and ye shall receive the gift of the Holy Ghost."* There is a reason for repentance. There is a reason—a specific purpose—for being water baptized in the name of Jesus Christ, and there is a reason you need the baptism of the Holy Ghost, God in you!

The reason is that you must be born again!

Discerning Good and Evil—Part 1

"For when for the time ye ought to be teachers, ye have need that one teach you again which be the first principles of the oracles of God; and are become such as have need of milk, and not of strong meat. For every one that suet milk is unskillful in the word of righteousness: for he is a babe. But strong meat belongeth to them that are of full age, even those who by reason of use have their senses exercised to discern both good and evil" (Hebrews 5:12-14).

This Scripture states that a person who is strong in the Lord is a person who can discern between good and evil. Every Christian should be able to discern and make proper decisions between good and bad, right and wrong, or to use an Old Testament phrase, the holy and the profane.

All things are not good. Some things are evil. Sin is not relative to circumstances. Fundamental morality never changes. Generation after generation can base their lives on the same truths. Truth is truth.

Yet we live in a world that is teaching our children that there are no absolutes: no black and white. This is taught in our schools and colleges to the point where a God-fearing, Bible-believing, fundamental Christian is looked upon as out-of-step and out of sync with the modern world in which we live.

God's people will not be politically correct. **We need to be Biblically correct!**

The spirit of Antichrist is a deceiving spirit. To be deceived is to err in your heart (See Hebrews 3:10). **I believe that much of the testing that Christians are facing today is to test our ability to discern the difference between good and bad.** For example, Former President Barrack Obama made this statement in a speech given to a church. "We are no longer a Christian nation; we are now a nation of Christians, Jews, Muslims and Buddhists."

Yet, history proves that America was founded as a Christian nation and a vast majority of Americans still claim to be Christians.

Mr. Obama went on to further state that it's wrong to legislate any laws that would offend any religion, including atheists. In other words, no law should be passed in America that offends anyone's religion, including those who do not believe in a God. Is there anyone reading this who discerns that this thinking, this world view, this pluralistic humanist philosophy is bad, not good? Can we discern that it is profane, not holy?

William Booth, founder of the Salvation Army said this: "The chief danger of the 20th century will be religion without the Holy Spirit, Christianity without Christ, forgiveness without repentance, salvation without regeneration, politics without God, and heaven without hell." We can see that he was exactly right. Too many Christians, let alone secular humanists, cannot discern between good and bad, right and wrong, or the holy and profane.

It's time that we wake up, America! It's time to evangelize the Jews, the Muslims, and the Buddhists. We are not to compromise with their idols and false teachings. Acts 2:38 is still relevant to this generation. Let's preach it till Jesus comes!

Discerning Good and Evil—Part 2

"But strong meat belongeth to them that are of full age, even those who by reason of use have their senses exercised to discern both good and evil" (Hebrews 5:14). I have expressed to you that too many Christians, let alone secular humanists, can't discern between right and wrong, good and bad, the holy and the profane.

Isn't that a major problem today? Our society has been taken over with the political correctness syndrome to the point that it is now improper to offend anyone by our beliefs, especially if we are Christians. It's almost political suicide to be vocal about being a fundamental, evangelical, conservative Christian. It seems to be okay to be a liberal Christian with no convictions. But, a conservative Christian with rock solid principles is seen as hardheaded, stiff-necked, unloving, and judgmental.

I agree we have to be careful about having a Pharisee's attitude of pride and arrogance. I agree that we will be judged by that with which we judge. I am not your final judge. But, liberal Christians have taken this idea to such an extreme that it seems that no one will stand up and say the obvious when there is wrongdoing, sin, or false doctrine for fear of offending someone.

I well remember back in the late 60's when the Jesus Movement came along. It was radical. It threw away any kind of judgment, or should I say discernment. Fearful lest someone would question a person's

135

faith, all kinds of ungodliness, perversion, lewdness, provocative dress, you name it, was allowed into many churches in the name of tolerance. But, wait a moment! Sin is sin. Evil is evil. I don't care how you dress it or what you call it. If you are living with someone, having intimate relationship with someone, who is not your spouse in the sight of God or the land, you are committing fornication. Can you not discern between right and wrong**? Do you think you can hide from God's presence, or think that He cannot see you?**

There is an interesting Scripture in Haggai chapter 1, verses 6 -7, "*Ye have sown much, and bring in little; ye eat, but ye have not enough; ye drink, but ye are not filled with drink; ye clothe you, but there is none warm; and he that earneth wages earneth wages to put it into a bag with holes. Thus saith the LORD of hosts; Consider your ways.*"

When you live in sin, things do not go well. You may have seasons of prosperity and times of wellness, but sin brings destruction of body, soul and spirit. So, when things are going bad; when you sow much and bring in little; you drink but you are not filled; you earn wages and put it into a bag with holes, you are cursed with a curse and God is trying to talk to you.

The Lord said, "*consider your ways.*" The Amplified Version says "*consider how you have fared.*" And, I'm not talking about your bank account necessarily. How are you faring? Consider your ways. How have you been living? What have you been doing? How have you been acting?

You'd better learn the difference between right and wrong, good and bad. It's the difference between heaven and hell.

Healing and Deliverance

"The Spirit of the Lord is upon me, because he hath anointed me to preach the gospel to the poor; he hath sent me to heal the broken-hearted, to preach deliverance to the captives, and recovering of sight to the blind, to set at liberty them that are bruised" (Luke 4:18).

Christ's purpose for coming to the earth has never changed. This is what He did during his 3½ years of ministry as recorded in Matthew, Mark, Luke, and John. The poor had the gospel preached to them. The brokenhearted found healing. The captives were delivered by the preaching of deliverance. The blinded eyes were opened. And those who were bruised found incredible liberty. It's irrelevant whether you take this statement literally, spiritually, physically or metaphorically. God worked miracles in people's lives! Lives that were physically, spiritually or emotionally hurting.

A woman came to church Wednesday night with an ankle so sore she couldn't stand on it. After church, she noticed, with thanksgiving, that there was no more pain. Her ankle had been healed during the service. She had received a miracle of physical healing! When you walk into a church where the Spirit of the Lord is invited and expected, anything can happen! Healing and deliverance is God's plan for a hurting world.

There are a lot of people who are disappointed with church because it has not been able to deliver what has been promised. People need more than a social activity. We need more than the respect of being a member of an established church. We all need more than 45 minutes of rituals, cute stories, and a showcase for our pretty clothes. We all need a visitation of God. **We need guidance, direction, healing, deliverance, peace of mind, and spiritual power to overcome the enemy of our soul.**

When the Lord said that He came to preach, heal, deliver, recover, and set at liberty, He didn't just mean for His short earthly ministry. Notice how the Lord addresses the Apostles and includes ALL believers!

"Afterward he appeared unto the eleven as they sat at meat, and upbraided them with their unbelief and hardness of heart, because they believed not them which had seen him after he was risen. And he said unto them, Go ye into all the world, and preach the gospel to every creature. He that believeth and is baptized shall be saved; but he that believeth not shall be damned. And these signs shall follow them that believe; In my name shall they cast out devils; they shall speak with new tongues; They shall take up serpents; and if the drink any deadly thing, it shall not hurt them; they shall lay hands on the sick, and they shall recover. So then after the Lord had spoken unto them, he was received up into heaven, and sat on the right hand of God. And they went forth, and preached everywhere, the Lord working with them, and confirming the word with signs following. Amen" (Mark 16:14-20).

On the Day of Pentecost it is very clear that not only were the Apostles filled with the Holy Ghost, but other disciples were filled also, numbering about 120, including Mary, the mother of Jesus. Yes, she needed to be born again of the water and the Spirit according to John chapter three.

The fact is that God is still working through His Spirit in believers today to bring to pass His ministry upon this earth. The heavens are being opened and there is an awareness of the presence of God as the powers of Satan are being rebuked and he is being put in his place of subjection to the Spirit of God. It is the business of the church to bind the powers of darkness that rule in the affairs of worldly men, so that the will of God can be done in this present day!

Three Types of Laws

The Scripture is adamant about the necessity of being obedient to God's laws. If we are to have peace with God, our Maker, we must adhere to His laws.

God's grace does not eliminate the need for that truth.

Titus 2:11-12, *"For the grace of God that bringeth salvation hath appeared to all men, Teaching us that, denying ungodliness and worldly lusts, we should live soberly, righteously, and godly, in this present world."*

God's grace will teach us to obey God's laws!

These are the principles that we find in God's laws. In the Old Testament, they were rules to be enforced. In the New Testament, Spirit-filled church, the laws become written in our hearts, and now we obey, not as by the letter, but by the Spirit within us.

So, the difficulty for some is in the application. How do we apply God's grace in practical living?

There are three types of laws recorded in the Bible. First of all, there are the civil laws. These are the laws of government. These are laws to be obeyed for the protection and the very peace of our lives. These laws can change with different people in power. But, they are basically for our good. **Civil laws can change.**

Then, there are the ceremonial laws, or the laws given for instruction in worship. God gave Moses and the children of Israel hundreds of laws that had to be kept if they wanted the blessing of God upon their lives, and many of these laws had to do with how God expected to be worshiped! Read, especially in Deuteronomy, the sundry laws pertaining to the sacrifice of animals, the duties of the priests, the ritual of worship, the keeping of holy days. These Old Testament ceremonial laws have been changed through the gospel of Jesus Christ. There is a great difference between worshiping God in the Old Testament and worshiping God in the New Testament.

For example, Jesus told the woman at the well, *"But the hour cometh, and now is, when the true worshippers shall worship the Father in spirit and in truth: for the Father seeketh such to worship him. God is a Spirit: and they that worship him must worship him in spirit and in truth"* (John 4:23-24).

What a difference! What a change! From ritualistic ceremonies to a Spirit-led worship from the heart! **Ceremonial laws have changed!** We no longer worship as the Old Testament saints did. Jesus became the Lamb that was slain and took our place in punishment.

But, there is a third type of law. That is the moral law. **Moral laws never change!** What was immoral in the Old Testament is still immoral in the New Testament. The sins of mankind today are the same as they were in the Garden of Eden.

"For all that is in the world, the lust of the flesh, and the lust of the eyes, and the pride of life, is not of the Father, but is of the world" (I John 2:16).

A lie is still a lie. Stealing is still stealing. Fornication is still fornication. Adultery is still a sin, etc.

Somehow, someway, Western society has come to believe that if things are accepted socially, then God understands and winks at abominations. Sorry, folks, but that is simply not so. There's going to be a lot of surprises when the Lord comes back for His Church and only the obedient, the faithful and the holy will be caught away.

Believing in God without works to accompany faith is not believing. People have been taught a lie, and want to believe it because it is convenient today. Faith without works is dead; useless; of no value. Faith without works will not produce the desired results in a person's life when Jesus comes back for His Church.

Moral laws never change.

Man has to change, for and by the grace of God!

Devils Tremble

The Bible says that at the knowledge of the fact that there is one God, the devil and all of his demons tremble. Let's read the Scripture in James 2:19: *"Thou believest that there is one God; thou doest well: the devils also believe, and tremble."* We need to get the setting for this verse. James is teaching here about the necessity of proving your faith by your works.

Let's read the whole setting. James 2: 17-20, *"Even so faith, if it hath not works, is dead, being alone. Yea, a man may say, Thou hast faith, and I have works: shew me thy faith without thy works, and I will shew thee my faith by my works. Thou believest that there is one God; thou doest well: the devils also believe, and tremble. But wilt thou know, O vain man, that faith without works is dead?"*

What the Apostle of our Lord is saying here is that you think because you believe in God that will save you. He says, no, even the devils have that knowledge, but they sure aren't saved. It's right that we believe in God, One God, he says, but let's also understand that Satan and his demons have such faith that they tremble. The Greek, for the word translated tremble, means to bristle, to chill, to shudder. Understand this: **The very knowledge of one God causes Satan to have cold chills. It causes his hair to stand up (if he has hair!). This knowledge causes all the devilish inhabitants of hell to shake and tremble.**

143

Let's go a little further. How is this knowledge of God transferred to Satan? Here's how! God is represented on earth by the followers of Jesus Christ. God's power in dealing with mankind is manifested through His Church, His real Church, His Holy Church, not necessarily all of the visible church, you understand, but rather that Church that is blood-bought, redeemed by the blood, sanctified; has taken on His name in a watery grave of baptism, and has been filled with the Holy Spirit, the Holy Ghost and fire. That's the Church that can proclaim the name of Jesus Christ, the only saving name in the universe!

Acts 4:12, *"Neither is there salvation in any other: for there is none other name under heaven given among men, whereby we must be saved."*

These are the people of the name; the people that not only know the name, but live out the saving power of God in their lives. When these people call on the name of Jesus, the devils tremble, they shiver with fear because they recognize that that name can render them powerless.

Throughout the gospels, demons cried out in fear when Jesus even approached or got near them. They cried to be left alone. Why? Because they knew the power of God.

Oh, friends, how I wish there were more that recognized that power and were willing to live their life so that that power could be manifested among us to a greater measure. Jesus called us His witnesses. He called us the salt and light of the world. He called us to preach the gospel to every creature. God is manifested through His Church. If devils are going to tremble at the knowledge of God, then it will be through people, human beings like you and me, that have that kind of relationship with God where the devils take notice and back off.

I'm fed up with Satan and his devilish forces ruling the lives of so many that I come in contact with. There are too many people walking the streets of our communities, going to our schools, working in our workplaces, even attending our churches that need set free from the bondage of Satan. **Truth that doesn't set you free is not truth!**

Let me give you a little insight into what is happening in America right now. We all know that America was founded on Christian principles. For about 200 years, these principles held true. The majority of Americans had a worldview that honored the Bible, and honored the name of Jesus Christ. But, during the time of our bicentennial, 1976, there was a great revolution going on in America, a great rebellion by learned men and women, by secular scholars who thought they knew better and they decided that America would be a better country if we laid aside the Biblical worldview that had brought us to where we were. Up until this time, as a whole, as a corporate entity, America was blessed by God, and Satan trembled, and had to back off in trying to curse America. America was blessed.

But over the last 40+ years, the church, supposedly the manifestation of God on Earth, has fallen away from its Biblical moorings and allowed the world to get into the church. The church world as a whole, as a corporate body, is so worldly, so carnal, so backslidden, that when they call on the name of God, it's only in ritualistic acts with no spiritual power and no corresponding results in the spirit world.

How sad. How tragic. We've seen what the result of an absence of God has done for other nations that have rejected the Christian faith. Atheistic nations have been ruled by dictators and ungodly men that have murdered millions in their search for power. Nations that have worshiped other gods, such as the Hindus with their hundreds of gods, have experienced extreme poverty, disease, government corruption, and harsh government controls. Demon possession is rampant in those nations, because there is no widespread knowledge of God.

We in America are now seeing more demon possession, devil worship, more occult activity; not because the devil is stronger, no…the church is weaker!

America is beginning to reap the whirlwind of vices that she has endorsed. Today's government is an embarrassment to right thinking citizens. The corruption, the lies (which are now called misrepresentations), the greed, the manipulation…all of this is being displayed every day in the media.

145

Folks, in regards to our nation, I'm afraid the devil is no longer trembling, but laughing. All because of a worldview that has dismissed the power of the name of our God; because of a worldview of New Age thinking; because of a worldview of appeasement. **You can't appease the devil.** The only way that a war is won is for one side to defeat the other! Whether through military might or diplomatic channels, someone has got to win!

I read a yard sign the other day that said, "Prayer, America's only hope." And, that's good. I certainly agree.

But, let's take it a step further. I say "Repentance, America's only hope."

After 9-11, signs went up everywhere that said, "God bless America." Yes, we certainly need God's blessings, but the way to get those blessings is to repent of our sins! Repentance will bring about a spiritual power, a righteous relationship with God that will cause the devil to tremble when we pray. It will cause the devil to tremble when we worship. It will cause the devil to tremble when we start witnessing to someone. Why? Because a person, as a born again child of God, represents God on this earth. We are His ambassadors (see II Corinthians 5:20).

Let's make Jesus Christ the Lord over our lives and our land. The devil will be shaking in his boots, his hair will stand on end, and the glory of God will be revealed in people's lives, instead of destruction, hatred, violence, sin, and unrighteousness.

A Dilemma or a Predicament

From a message by Rev. C.B. Burkett, Tiptonville, TN

(Used by permission)

Two hunters came across a bear so big that they dropped their rifles and ran for cover. One man climbed a tree while the other hid in a nearby cave. The bear was in no hurry to eat, so he sat down between the tree and the cave to reflect upon his good fortune. Suddenly, and for no apparent reason, the hunter in the cave came rushing out, almost ran into the waiting bear, hesitated, and then dashed back in again. The same thing happened the second time. When he emerged for the third time, his companion in the tree frantically called out, "Woody, are you crazy? Stay in the cave till he leaves!"

"Can't," panted Woody, "there's another bear in there."

That's a dilemma!

A dilemma is a situation requiring a choice between equally un-desirable alternatives. A dilemma has no good answer. There is no possibility of a good outcome. If the hunter stayed in the cave, there was a bear there. If he ran out, there was a bear there. Both wanted him for their dinner. That's a dilemma.

On the other hand a predicament is an unpleasantly difficult, per-plexing or dangerous situation.

What would you call the story of David and Goliath? A dilemma for David? On the surface it looked like David was walking into a dilemma. No good way out. He was challenging the giant but common sense said there was no real, positive way out of the situation. That's a dilemma.

But, David looked upon it as a predicament—just an unpleasant, dangerous situation. His brothers, along with King Saul, and all the other soldiers who had been fearful of this giant surely looked upon this situation as a dilemma. Young David has good intentions, but he is in a dilemma. There is surely no way out of this confrontation. But, David saw it as a predicament not a dilemma!

How about your situation today? Are you facing a dilemma or a predicament? Sort of depends how you are looking at it, doesn't it? You may be facing a situation and feel like there is no good way out—that there is no acceptable answer to your problem. A dilemma brings despair, hopelessness, and fear, even suicide. A dilemma causes a person to give up. A dilemma also puts God out of the picture.

Hear me now. **God has never faced a dilemma!** Predicaments, yes, but never a dilemma. There has never been a time when God didn't know what to do. He even knows what to do about your situation today! You don't, but He does! God is not scratching His head wondering how to get you out of the mess you've created. All He is doing is waiting on you to humble yourself before Him in sincere repentance and acknowledge that He is in control of your life. *"Ask and you shall receive. Seek and ye shall find. Knock and it shall be opened unto you"* (Matthew 7:7). God is waiting on you. Looking at your problem as a predicament gives God an opportunity to work!

In St John chapter 8 we have the story of the woman taken in adultery. The religious authorities brought her to Jesus to see what He would do in punishment. The Jewish law stated that she should be stoned to death. She knew this law just like the Lord knew it. What a dilemma! She was caught in the act of sin with a stated judgment already written in the law. There was to be no trial. It was over: a dilemma; no way out; no excuse; no pleading with a judge; just certain death.

But, the scribes and Pharisees had brought her to Jesus. Isn't that beautiful? **If you can just get to Jesus, your dilemma can be turned into a predicament.** The dilemma said you are to die. The Lord turned the same situation into a predicament. After writing in the sand He asked that those without sin would cast the first stone. And one by one, all of her accusers went away. What an unbelievable turn of events. Just a few minutes before, she was to die. A dilemma is now, just a predicament. Just go and sin no more. What a beautiful picture of grace…of God's love. The Lord didn't justify her sin. He didn't tell her it was OK. He just gave her another chance!

Can you turn your dilemmas over to the Lord? If so, there is hope! There will be a tomorrow. There will be a fresh anointing if you will submit yourself to the potter's wheel and let the Lord work on you for a while.

Jairus' daughter was sick unto death. He had heard of the healing power of this man named Jesus. One day, he got to where Jesus was, they talked and the Lord was willing to come to his house. But, on the way, the lady with the issue of blood delayed the Lord's arrival at Jairus' house and a servant came to announce that his daughter was dead. The first words out of the Lord's mouth were these: *"Fear not, believe only and she shall be made whole"* (Luke 8:50). Let's rephrase that. **Don't believe that this is a dilemma with no way out. This is just a predicament.** And, if you will believe, your daughter will live again. Jesus simply took her by the hand and said *"Maid arise"* (Luke 8:54).

Is this not a wonderful lesson for someone today? The Holy Ghost has sent these words to you today, to tell you that your dilemma is just a predicament. I'm not belittling your predicament. I'm sure it's mind-blowing serious. You may be facing a complete lifestyle change through a devastating sickness or disease. Maybe it's the loss of a loved one, a divorce, a child that has wandered from God or a financial disaster that has you feeling closed in on every side.

God has never seen a dilemma. Even when Adam and Eve failed, He already had a plan. Even when King Saul failed, God had a plan. When the three Hebrew children were thrown into the fiery furnace,

God was not stymied on how to get them out. He just joined them in the fire! Wow! Did you get that? God just joined them in the fire!

I can speak from experience today. My greatest spiritual growth has come during times when the flesh thought I was in a dilemma. But, knowing the Word of God, I refused to bow to those feelings. I called on God. He came through. He always does. When I saw God turn my dilemma into a predicament my faith was increased and I'm stronger today than I was before my predicament. Trust Him. He cares. Let Him turn your dilemma into a predicament.

Generational Curses

After the great faith chapter of Hebrews 11, the next chapter starts off like this. Hebrews 12:1, *"Wherefore seeing we also are compassed about with so great a cloud of witnesses, let us lay aside every weight, and the sin which doth so easily beset us, and let us run with patience the race that is set before us."* **Too often people are not able to run the spiritual race that is set before them, because of besetting sins and heavy weights.**

A besetting sin is one that we just can't resist—a sin that we can't seem to get the victory over. A person may have prayed, made vows to God and promises to his family that he would change. However, there are some sins that just come so naturally and they easily beset us. In other words, they overtake us easily. From destructive addictions to bondage through abominations, too many people's lives are trapped in a never ending circle of destruction and even death. The thought of suicide is not even out of the question to some as a way to escape the never ending failures and down-fallings. Many have tried religion even going from church to church trying to find an answer. Others are often flipping through the channels on Christian broadcasting trying to find someone with a word from God for them.

I have found that those who are suffering with this kind of a spiritual problem are often affected by generational bondage; bondage and sins that have been passed down from previous generations in their family.

Can you think of a problem you're having now that your father, mother, or other family members have suffered with also? Many times, this is the case. Drug addicts beget drug addicts. Alcoholics beget alcoholics. Worriers beget worriers. Feelings and emotions such as fear, rejection, and inferiority complexes are things that we pass from generation to generation. Professional counselors tell us that if a person beats his or her child, that child will beat his or her child.

The Bible says in Exodus 34:7 that the iniquities of our fathers are passed down to the 3rd and 4th generation. There are numerous other Scriptures that bear this out. Note that iniquities are generally defined as moral sin or sins of character, such as rejection of God, immorality, perversion, and a disregard of God.

But, let me take you to the answer today.

When the children of Israel were ready to go into the promise land, Canaan, God told them to prepare themselves by repenting of their sins: not only their sins, but also for the iniquities of their fathers. (Read it in Leviticus 26:40.) **We know that repentance is the gateway to God.** Not just believing on the Lord, but repenting of sins is a prerequisite for spiritual life. Not just sorrow. Repentance is the fruit of Godly sorrow (II Cor. 7:10).

"Repent ye therefore, and be converted, that your sins may be blotted out, when the times of refreshing shall come from the presence of the Lord"(Acts 3:9). The revised version, and the vast majority of other versions, state that the Scripture is saying repent and be converted so that the times of refreshing shall come from the presence of the Lord. **We don't repent when the refreshing comes. We repent so the refreshing will come!**

But, many have never experienced the liberty and bondage-breaking power that comes when they confess the sins of those who have sinned against them. No, you can't save them, but you can break the generational bondage, (generational curses) by repenting for *their* sins that have affected you down through the years. It's like a circuit breaker in what we used to call a fuse box. You break the connection with your past when you repent for the sins of the past. It's much like the power of repenting for the sins of the land. Jeremiah and Daniel repented for the sins of their land. We are also told to repent for the iniquities of our fathers!

I'm trying to tell someone that there is hope. You don't have to go on suffering guilt and defeat because of the sins of your fathers, or your family that are binding you. Repent! Tell God that you are sorry for what your father did to you. Tell God that you are sorry for what your mother did to you through her sins. Tell God that you are repenting for lifestyles that left God out of your life. This step cannot be taken in anger or bitterness. This doesn't necessarily mean that you didn't have good parents—even Christian parents. But, if something from your upbringing has caused you to say, "I'll never be different because this is the way my dad did it," or "this is the way my mother lived," I'm here to tell you there is great power in the repentance of our father's sins.

Why does repentance work? Repentance is God's way for you and me to enter into His presence. Repentance is the conception of spiritual life just like conception starts natural life. Likewise, water baptism is like a baby in the womb and the first thing after delivery is the breath of life, likened to the infilling of the Holy Ghost in the life of a believer.

Repentance can and will break the bondage of witchcraft, sorcery, sexual and moral perversion; the bondage of the gay lifestyle, lesbianism, and the rampant sins of fornication and adultery in our generation. How can it be that half of those who get married today, have lived together in sin first, often even having children before marriage, with no social reprimand, and hardly a reprimand from the Church and often with the approval of many parents considering such abomination as normal for our day. Folks, it's time to realize that we don't have to go on with such wickedness. Much of this has been handed down from generation to generation. Children have grown up with several people filling the role of daddy or mommy in their life. Children have seen mother go into her bedroom with numerous men. No wonder there is an abundance of generational curses today!

The Lord has sent me to you to tell you that you can get on your knees with heartfelt repentance for your sins and the sins of your fathers and you can break that bondage in a supernatural demonstration of God's power in your life. God is real. And, His forgiveness is real. God loves you!

Iniquities of the Fathers

Let's examine a parable together.

Sam comes to church and finds an experience with God that is quickly noticed by his family and co-workers. There certainly has been a change in Sam.

But soon Sam realizes that he still has a strong attraction to his old addiction of abusing prescription drugs. Somehow, someway, that problem that Sam had hoped would disappear was still there. Sam's wife can't believe that he is still struggling and still ruining the family budget with this addiction—this same addiction that has ruined their marriage with years of struggle and has even brought on physical attacks. Despite his confession of conversion, there is something drastically wrong.

I use this parable to share with you what I've seen happen in people's lives. I've preached for years that when you get saved, you're free from addictions, bondages, sins. I believe there is power in the blood of Jesus Christ to fulfill those declarations. But, more often than we want to admit, the worst cases of bondage sometimes leave our altars still bound and still hindered and I have been seeking the face of God for an answer. **Show me, God, what I need to know to break through the spiritual bondage that is prevalent in so many people's lives.**

Let me share with you some Scriptures that might help us to find an answer. The Bible clearly states, that "the iniquity of our fathers is visited upon the children unto the third and fourth generations. *"Keeping mercy for thousands, forgiving iniquity and transgression and sin, and that will by no means clear the guilty; visiting the iniquity of the fathers upon the children, and upon the children's children, unto the third and to the fourth generation"* (Exodus 34:7).

I want to say first of all that there are generational blessings as well as generational curses! I have been blessed to have been brought up in a home where the fear of God was taught and going to church was our lifestyle. My parents raised me and my two brothers in a Christian environment and I am forever thankful! I have experienced generational blessings and I owe a big thanks to my mom and dad.

But I am aware that many others have experienced generational bondage or curses. The sins, that fathers (i.e. families) have been in bondage to, will be felt and lived out by their children, down to the fourth generation. What you do today affects your children tomorrow. And, of course, if someone doesn't break that generational bondage, then that cycle will just continue generation after generation. Alcoholics beget alcoholics. Drug addicts beget drug addicts. Homes with no fear of God beget homes with no fear of God.

Notice in this Scripture that there are three categories of sins mentioned; iniquities, transgressions, and sins.

Go back to the original Hebrew and you will find that an iniquity is a moral evil or perversity which is a sin of character against the nature of God. People are guilty of iniquity when they disregard God. Look how many families are raised with no regard to God in their lives! How many children have been raised with apparent approval of sexual sins, including fornication and adultery, both of which are iniquities? Parents who are involved in such sins have a real problem trying to teach their children not to commit those same sins.

A transgression is a rebellion or trespass; to knowingly do wrong.

And, a definition of the word sin is missing the mark or falling short of the mark.

Let me summarize. **To sin is to fall short of the mark. To transgress is to knowingly do wrong. And, an iniquity is a moral sin that is in the character of a person.**

Please follow me closely here. I believe that a sin or a transgression can be corrected by anyone who wants to quit sinning. Just stop missing the mark and just stop breaking God's laws. This is possible through sincere repentance, self discipline, and a made up mind to serve the Lord.

But, an iniquity can be deeper than that. God says that, not transgressions or sins, but iniquities are visited upon the 3rd and 4th generations. Why? Iniquities involve character. Iniquities often involve a person's culture.

Iniquities are the types of sins that people find it hard to break. A person raised in a drug environment must break generational bondage to be free spiritually. Sometimes this happens at the moment of repentance. Thank God for those glorious times! And, I've seen it happen many times in my ministry. But, to be honest, there have been other times where I've seen people struggle for years with these curses from their past still binding them.

How does a person break them? Obviously repentance is needed. But, notice with me in Leviticus 26:40. When Israel is getting ready to cross into Canaan, God tells them how they will obtain victory. They must confess their iniquity, and the iniquity of their fathers. Here God gives us the key to spiritual victory over the sins of our fathers. Repent for the iniquities of our fathers. **Not only are we to repent for our sins, but we are to repent for the sins of our family that haunt us.** And, there are scriptural examples of this happening. In Daniel 9:20, Daniel prayed for his sin and the sin of his people. The prophet Jeremiah acknowledged his generation's sins and the iniquity of their fathers in Jeremiah 14:20.

There is so much more to this message of deliverance. I hope I've said enough to get you to search the Scriptures and see whether these things be so. I'm telling you that I believe there is hope for every person who feels they are trapped in generational curses, through obedience to the Word of God, by sincerely repenting of your own sins, and also repenting for the iniquities of your fathers. You can't save them. They will have to save themselves. But, you can break the generational bondage and cross into the promise land victorious and free from bondage.

The Captive Can be Set Free

It may be as simple as recurring guilt or a never ending fear. It may be the pain of a failed relationship or the ongoing depression that seldom lets up. Or, it may be the destructive behavior that you've tried for too long to break away from, but all too often, you find yourself saying you're sorry again and again.

Most alcoholics I've dealt with are so sorry after the binge. Drug addicts eventually will yearn for deliverance. Every addicted mother is so sorry for what is happening to her children and every spouse is terrified as to what is happening to their marriage. How many have I talked to that have been through rehab, professional counseling, or even jail time and vow over and over that this time will be different.

The power of the gospel of Jesus Christ is to set the captive free!

And, don't think that "jail house religion" can't be real. I've learned that many do find help while incarcerated. Thank God for the victories and for the men and women with compassion to reach those who are incarcerated.

But, I've also seen the vows that had been made to man and God, broken within minutes of walking out of jail. Promises are shattered. Lives continue their headlong plunge into dismal failure. Money that was needed so desperately for food, shelter, clothing, medicine, and other necessities, gone in a moment for a quick fix of a drink or drug.

There has got to be a deliverance from bondage and a deliverance from sin. Often what is needed is a deliverance from generational curses. Is that possible?

But, let me change the picture a moment. Let's walk in a church. Here are people, good people, good moral people, trying their best to live for God. People who love God, love doing good, love their families, and love their church family. But, far too many walk out of the church building day after day, month after month, year after year, battling the same battles, waging the same warfare, feeling trapped and hopeless over perhaps only one or two situations, but nevertheless, hopeless. Recurring sins, recurring bad habits, uncontrolled lust of the flesh, lust of the eyes, pride of life, all that's in the world (See I John 2:16). Yes, they have allowed God to do some wonderful things in their lives. But still it is there. It haunts them to the point that they sooner or later just give up trying to overcome and assume they are going to have to live with this problem the rest of their lives.

I'm talking about problems that hinder the quality of life; problems and feelings that come between them and others. Secret sins that they would be embarrassed of if anyone knew they committed.

Several years ago in Indiana, our family was ministering in a church and the pastor pointed out a certain woman in the congregation and then told me this story about her conversion. She had made a counseling appointment with a denominational pastor in this particular town, and she told him that she was a lesbian, alcoholic, etc., possibly demon possessed. The denominational pastor just looked at her for a moment and then said, **"I can't help you here. But, if you'll go down the street a couple of blocks and turn left, you'll find a Pentecostal church. They can help you."** She did. And, they did!

It takes the power of the experience of Pentecost—the indwelling Spirit of God, the Holy Ghost, to save souls. That's the power to set you free! Power to turn your life around!

"But ye shall receive power, after that the Holy Ghost is come upon you" (Acts 1:8).

Jesus is still the answer!

"The Spirit of the Lord is upon me, because he hath anointed me to preach the gospel to the poor; he hath sent me to heal the broken-hearted, to preach deliverance to the captives, and recovering of sight to the blind, to set at liberty them that are bruised (Luke 4:18).

Be filled with the Spirit!

This is STILL That

Joel had prophesied about the pouring out of the Spirit of God upon humanity and about a time when God's laws would be written in men's hearts and they could be led by the Spirit of God. Joel 2: 28-29, *"And it shall come to pass afterward, that I will pour out my spirit upon all flesh; and your sons and your daughters shall prophesy, your old men shall dream dreams, your young men shall see visions: And also upon the servants and upon the handmaids in those days will I pour out my spirit."*

God used the prophet Joel to tell of a coming day when all flesh, sons and daughters, old men and young men, would be supernaturally filled with the Spirit of God and would supernaturally speak God's Word, dream and see visions.

From the time of his writings, let's move forward some 800 years. Fifty days after Passover, the Jews were celebrating a feast day—the day of Pentecost—a feast commemorating the giving of the law on Mt. Sinai. Jesus had told His disciples in Luke 24:49, *"And, behold, I send the promise of my Father upon you: but tarry ye in the city of Jerusalem, until ye be endued with power from on high."* So, after the Lord's ascension, the disciples had waited some ten days on the promise of the Father.

Acts 2:*1-4, "And when the day of Pentecost was fully come, they were all with one accord in one place. And suddenly there came a sound from heaven as of a rushing mighty wind, and it filled all the house where they were sitting. And there appeared unto them cloven tongues like as of fire, and it sat upon each of them. And they were all filled with the Holy Ghost, and began to speak with other tongues, as the Spirit gave them utterance."*

Look what the wind blew in!

This same experience is the normal experience for the New Testament church today! While some say that I Corinthians 13 infers that spiritual gifts ceased when the Word of God was completed or at some other season in the early church, there are others of us who have simply received what is obviously promised. *"When that which is perfect is come"* (I Corinthians 13:10) refers to the Second Coming of Jesus Christ. So the gifts are still operating among those who have the faith to believe. Paul said in I Corinthians 12:1, *"Now concerning spiritual gifts, brethren, I would not have you ignorant."*

As Peter stood up and preached to the crowd on the day of Pentecost, he said in Acts 2:15-16, *"For these are not drunken, as ye suppose, seeing it is but the third hour of the day. But this is that which was spoken by the prophet Joel;"*

Folks, when the Spirit fell upon the day of Pentecost, the people were accused, by their actions, of being drunk. But, Peter shouted out, *"This is that spoken of by the Prophet Joel."* I want to tell someone that **This is STILL that!** As one preacher preached, **We ain't as drunk as we oughta be!!** Have you ever been drunk on the Spirit of God? Give me that old time religion, it's good enough for me!

A watered down, diluted, anemic, sterile gospel will not change people's lives. It can fill a church building, but it can't change a person's life. That kind of gospel won't bring about the desired results in deliverance from sin and bondage. A person who is truly born again will be radically changed! A new birth will result in a changed lifestyle.

2 Corinthians 5:17, *"Therefore if any man be in Christ, he is a new creature: old things are passed away; behold, all things are become*

new.'' Too many people settle for something less than a THIS IS THAT experience.

2 Timothy 3:5, *"Having a form of godliness, but denying the power thereof: from such turn away."*

In these final hours of mankind's world as we know it, the world needs this Pentecostal experience. I call it the Pentecostal experience because it's the same experience that the first church, on the day of Pentecost, the 120 in the upper room, received when Peter said, **This is That!** I'm preaching to you, that **this is STILL that! This supernatural, born again experience is STILL what God wants to do for any honest-hearted seeker! Be filled with the Spirit! Be filled with the Holy Ghost!**

The household of Cornelius were the first gentiles to receive eternal life. Acts 10: 44-46, *"While Peter yet spake these words, the Holy Ghost fell on all them which heard the word. And they of the circumcision which believed were astonished, as many as came with Peter, because that on the Gentiles also was poured out the gift of the Holy Ghost. For they heard them speak with tongues, and magnify God."*

Peter and his entire group knew that the household of Cornelius had received the same gift as the Jews at Pentecost, because they heard them speak with tongues and magnify God!

This is STILL that! Don't let anyone take this truth from you!

Works Cited

Blackaby, Henry, and Claude King. *Experiencing God.*

Nashville: Lifeway, 1990. Print.

Pierce, Chuck. *Interpreting the Times.* Lake Mary, Florida.

Charisma House. 2008. Print.

Labberton, Mark. *The Dangerous Act of Worship.* Downers

Grove, IL. IVP Books. 2012. Print.

Strong's Concordance Greek 5198

Grady, Lee. "The Fire of Holiness vs. The Spirit of Perversion." *Charismamag.com.* Charisma Magazine. 29 September, 2010. Web. 20 June, 2016. charismamag.com/blogs/fire-in-my-bones/11900-the-fire-of-holiness-vs-the-spirit-of-perversion.

Spiritual Warfare in the Kingdom of Skullbonia

greenfieldconnect.COM

LINKING YOU TO THE GREENFIELD EXPERIENCE

—— resources for YOU ——

FIRST UNITED PENTECOSTAL CHURCH OF GREENFIELD, TN

A SPIRIT—FILLED CHURCH PREACHING SALVATION, HEALING
AND DELIVERANCE.

SACKS THRIFT AVENUE / SACKS FOOD PANTRY

A COMMUNITY SUPPORTED THRIFT STORE AND AREA—WIDE FOOD PANTRY

THE HAVEN OF GREENFIELD, TENNESSEE

A TRANSITIONAL HOME FOR WOMEN

CELEBRATE RECOVERY

FREEDOM FROM HURTS, HANG—UPS AND HABITS WITH SMALL GROUP
MINISTRY AND ASSOCIATED JAIL MINISTRIES AND FOLLOW—UP

RADIO PROGRAM

REACHING THE WORLD THROUGH RADIO AND
ONLINE STREAMING EVERY SUNDAY

CONCERTS

CHURCH SERVICES

CAMP MEETINGS

REVIVALS

For product sales, schedule, and ministry information visit
THECHANDLERSMUSIC.COM

COPIES OF THIS BOOK MAY ALSO BE PURCHASED ONLINE

THE CHANDLERS | PO BOX 152, GREENFIELD, TN 38230 | (800) 214-6509